Caught Off Guard

Encounters
with the
Unexpected God

A series published in cooperation with
THE CHRISTIAN COUNSELING AND EDUCATIONAL FOUNDATION
Glenside, Pennsylvania

Susan Lutz, Series Editor

Other books by our authors:

Edward T. Welch, *When People Are Big and God Is Small: Overcoming Peer Pressure, Codependency, and the Fear of Man*, P&R Publishing

Paul David Tripp, *Age of Opportunity: A Biblical Guide to Parenting Teens*, P&R Publishing

Edward T. Welch, *Blame It on the Brain? Distinguishing Chemical Imbalances, Brain Disorders, and Disobedience*, P&R Publishing

James C. Petty, *Step by Step: Divine Guidance for Ordinary Christians*, P&R Publishing

Paul David Tripp, *War of Words: Getting to the Heart of Your Communication Struggles*, P&R Publishing

Edward T. Welch, *Addictions – A Banquet in the Grave: Finding Hope in the Power of the Gospel*, P&R Publishing

Paul David Tripp, *Instruments in the Redeemer's Hands: People in Need of Change Helping People in Need of Change*, P&R Publishing

David Powlison, *Seeing with New Eyes: Counseling and the Human Condition through the Lens of Scripture*, P&R Publishing

Edward T. Welch, *Depression – A Stubborn Darkness: Light for the Path*, New Growth Press

David Powlison, *Speaking Truth in Love: Counsel in Community*, New Growth Press

Timothy S. Lane and Paul David Tripp, *How People Change*, New Growth Press

Timothy S. Lane and Paul David Tripp, *Relationships – A Mess Worth Making*, New Growth Press

Christian Counseling &
Educational Foundation

RESTORING CHRIST *to* COUNSELING &
COUNSELING *to the* CHURCH

Caught Off Guard

Encounters
with the
Unexpected God

William P. Smith

New
Growth
Press

– to Sari –

You believe in me like no one else on earth;
and so this book belongs to you like it does to no other.

ACKNOWLEDGMENTS

My debts on this project run higher than I will be able to adequately realize or acknowledge.

The Christian Counseling & Educational Foundation provided the time, opportunities, and a sabbatical to develop this material. Thank you, John Bettler, for bringing me on board. Thanks especially to Ed Welch, Paul Tripp, and Tim Lane for their input and support. David Powlison, Winston Smith, and Mike Emlet provided early venues for sharing some of these thoughts. Thanks too to Jayne Clark, our publications department director, who was willing to take a chance on an untested author. Many others of our staff have encouraged me over the years by asking how things were going. I am truly grateful to work with such gifted and pastoral people.

Sam Andreas, Andy Hudson, Deb Michaud, Ray Cannata and the Black Rock Retreat Center invited me to share some of these ideas with their congregations. These are opportunities and friendships for which I am grateful. You have only increased my enthusiasm. My heartfelt thanks as well to my students over the years at Biblical and Westminster Theological Seminaries, who endured being guinea pigs yet provided enthusiastic support nonetheless.

I am especially indebted to a number of the people I've counseled over the years, whose faces hovered in front of my eyes as I wrote, informing how and what I've written. Thank you for allowing me to be part of your lives. I did seek permission from people whose stories I share here, although my children have wished for slightly greater editorial authority than I granted them.

Speaking of editors, Sue Lutz and Nick Darrell have been outstanding. They diligently labored to extract the point I was trying to make from all the unnecessary verbiage and convoluted sentence structures. This has produced a clean, direct – readable! – book. The fact that you, the reader, have fewer rabbit trails to follow and less rambling to endure is due entirely to their efforts. They make me sound better than I have any right to. Places where you feel detoured are most likely where I am acting AEA (against editorial advice).

New Growth Press has been nothing except enthusiastic. That encouragement has meant a lot to me down the final stretch. Thank you, Karen Jacklin and Mark Teears. Thanks as well to Joan Johnson and Punch Marketing.

Lastly, my deep appreciation to my family, both my larger, extended one who regularly have asked how writing was going, and especially my wife and children. They have responded to my regular preoccupation, testy absorption, and irritated rantings during the process with love that covers a multitude of sins. They've listened patiently as I've tried out ideas and gamely given me permission to publicly reflect on their lives.

Thank you all.

– William P. Smith

If you want to build a ship, don't drum up people to collect wood and don't assign them tasks and work, but rather teach them to long for the endless immensity of the sea.

Antoine de Saint-Exupery

contents

PREFACE

"Bill, I know it in my head, but not in my heart!" Maria described her frustration with the gap between what she knew about God and the Christian life and how she actually lived. Maria had been a Christian for nearly a decade. She loved Jesus and was active in her church. Yet too many times, all the good theology she knew did not seem to affect her life. Instead, she found herself doing and saying things that embarrassed her. She found it hard to care about people. And, hardest to admit, she did not find God as attractive as he was supposed to be. The Christian life just did not seem to work very well for her.

KNOWLEDGE THAT'S NOT LIVED

Maria is not alone. Many people have the same frustration. They know what is true, but for some reason the truths they know and love don't find their way into their daily life. Instead, their faith exists in a separate sphere from the daily grind of diapers and deadlines. The young woman who worries about her reputation can provide rich details about the blow it is to her ego to stuff envelopes for an advertising agency. Yet she never mentions the God who gave her that job and who intends to use it to challenge her fear of others' opinions.

Or consider the man who fears that powerful people will somehow hurt him and his family. It never occurs to him to bring this fear to Jesus and learn that Christ's love really does cast out fear. Instead he feverishly plans ways to limit his exposure to threatening people. He would be shocked to realize that in daily conversation he sounds like an atheist, making no reference to the Lord he prays to and serves.

This is my problem too. How is it that I can teach and counsel these things and yet hear my daughter say to me, "Daddy, how come you never talk about Jesus anymore but only what to do next to fix the house?" I too know it in my head, but not always in my heart.

No doubt there are times when you also experience the conflict between head and heart. You know that God and the things he says are good, yet you struggle to believe and obey him. Trusting him and responding righteously don't seem to make much sense in the moment of difficulty. For example, reacting defensively to a critical spouse seems more sensible than turning away wrath with a gentle answer. Slandering a coworker who has taken credit for your work beats turning the other cheek. Worrying about job security seems more appropriate than trusting

God to care more for you than for many sparrows. Your conscience tells you that what you are doing is wrong, but you can't stop yourself. You know it in your head, but not in your heart.

Let's put it slightly differently: Sometimes people know things *about* God more than they actually know him. They have correct information, but they know them in a Trivial Pursuit kind of way, as interesting factoids with little relevance to daily life. Our ability to answer questions about God increases as we attend church, small groups, and Sunday school, but our experience of God does not necessarily deepen. And whenever knowledge outstrips experience, it is useless in the face of life's difficulties.

Let me tell you about a friend of mine we'll call Ron. I've known Ron for nearly twenty years. We've lived in the same house, been in each other's weddings, and attend the same church. Ron is a terrific guy who married a wonderful lady. Together they lovingly parent their adopted children. He is an elder, mission trips leader, and former youth pastor. Because he connects with teens like few can, he is regularly welcomed into their homes and lives. Ron is a great guy, with a carefree, spontaneous side. His love for Jesus is easy to see.

Now you know some interesting – and true – things about my friend. But you don't know Ron. If you had a flat tire in the middle of the night an hour away from Ron's house, would you call him for help? Of course you wouldn't! He might be a great guy, but you don't know how he would respond to you. You have no personal knowledge of his heart, his attitude toward people in trouble, or his typical responses. You have only heard about him, so he wouldn't enter your mind if you needed help. You need a trusting relationship with him to have confidence in his help.

The same is true of our relationship with Christ. If all you know are interesting facts about him, he will not enter your mind when life's unpleasantness confronts you. At best, he will be a pleasant after-thought to bring you comfort, but not any kind of meaningful help.

For instance, some people talk about God's omnipotence, yet they have no confidence that he brings this power into their lives when they feel out of control. Others know and talk about how Jesus forgives sins, but they walk around with a guilt that never seems to go away. Still others answer correctly that he does not harbor grudges, but they are afraid to come to him after they have yelled at their kids for the forty-seventh time. They know he is a friend of sinners, but they don't have confidence that he wants to be their friend.

The things they know are correct, but it is a formal knowledge devoid of connections to real life. It's not the kind of knowledge they can base their life on. They don't have confidence that he is alive and active in their lives.

Now let me tell you about the time I had a tire and a spare tire go flat in the middle of the night. How, when I called Ron and got his answering machine, he called back almost immediately. How, without grumbling or hesitation, he got up and drove forty-five minutes to pick me up. How he greeted me with a smile, jollied me up with his infectious humor, and drove me another forty-five minutes home. How he graciously slept on my family's couch, took me to buy another tire the next morning, drove me back to my car, waited to see that everything was okay, and then returned home, happy to have helped.

Now you're starting to get a feeling for the man. Not only do you know interesting, abstract truths about him, you've heard what he is like when the pressure is on. You've seen how he treated me, which shows you his heart toward me when I'm in trouble. The next time you get in a jam, you may even think about my friend and wish that you knew someone like him.

But wait! What would happen if I told you three more stories about Ron gladly helping others – including someone he hardly knew? I would not simply tell you what he said or did, but I would also describe his concern for the people he helped. Then let's say I gave you Ron's phone number and promised that he would welcome your call. Now if you were in the Philadelphia area with car trouble, he just might come to your mind! Chances are you might even call him. Because you saw his heart in action for people in similar situations, you would begin to believe he might do the same for you. Seeing him as someone who did not turn others away would affect how you would reach out to him.

That's my hope for this book. I want to tell you stories about God that show you his heart for people in distress. I want you to see his concern for people in trouble – including those who have brought their problems on themselves. People who sin big, are scared of life, who resist wise counsel, who shy away from the Lord, and are angry with him. In short, people who have no reason to expect his mercy or help. Yet people who get what they don't deserve in a good sense, because God is so much better than any of us believe. Because they experience his goodness, these people's lives are radically changed. They have come to know it in their hearts, because they've seen his heart expressed in his actions.

My goal in this book is to flesh out our knowledge of God in the midst of daily struggles. I hope that you will see more deeply and clearly the wonderful grace and goodness of God. Instead of being vague generalities,

I hope that "grace" and "goodness" will develop richer content that impacts you, right in the middle of careers and groceries. As you see how God responds to difficult people, I hope you will understand how he will connect with you when you're in trouble.

As I have studied, written, and spoken about our very good God, a deeper, livelier confidence in this Redeemer has grown in my heart. I have been overwhelmed by how wonderful he really is. He is big enough even to handle a mess like me! In seminary, mature preachers admonish their students, "Preach grace until you get it." As I have worked on this book, I can affirm the value and wisdom of that admonition.

In her series of books on ancient Rome, Colleen McCullough sketches the budding romance between Julius Caesar's daughter Julia and Gnaeus Pompeius Magnus.[1] Magnus was the idol of his day, so renowned that many young women bought small plaster busts of him so that they might dream of him incessantly. In an attempt to forge an alliance with Magnus by marriage to his daughter, Caesar invited him for dinner. Julia appeared taken with Magnus, but afterward she went to her room and unaccountably, to Caesar's mind, threw her bust of Magnus into the trash as though she wanted nothing more to do with him. Crestfallen over this unexpected development, Caesar sought his mother's counsel. She rescued her son's dashed hopes by explaining that, far from wanting to rid herself of Magnus, Julia was no longer content to settle for a figurine. She wanted the real thing.

As you read this book and watch God come near his people, I hope that you too will crave the real thing. I hope that you will be less satisfied with talking theology and long instead to know this God who longs for you.

---

[1] Colleen McCullough, *Caesar's Women* (New York, NY: Avon Books, 1997) pp. 717-721, 770-777.

on your own

At the end of each chapter you will find questions designed to help you interact with what you've read. Since part of the heart-head disconnect stems from a failure to apply the knowledge of God we already have, I want to suggest ways to apply the thoughts to your life.

1   Begin by acknowledging to God that, in some areas, your knowledge of him is abstract and theoretical. It might be helpful to identify aspects of God's character that you find hard to grasp, such as his sovereignty, his goodness, his forgiveness, his mercy, or his justice.

2   Where do you have trouble connecting your faith to your life? For instance, does God form part of the picture when people sin against you, when your health is poor, when your plans are disrupted?

3   Rather than thinking about this by yourself, it may help to ask people who know you to point out the things that seem to upset you most easily, or the situations that cause you to struggle.

4   Ask Jesus to renew your desire to know him personally, not just talk about him. In prayer, consider how life might be different: "If I knew God more fully, then I might dare to . . . ."

Part I

God shows you his heart

To many people who struggle with knowing God, he seems cold, aloof, and impersonal. He seems to be a God of towering, transcendent might who neither notices their distress nor cares to act on their behalf. He is a God who can't be bothered with them because they've given him no good reason to get involved, a God who is only near and personal to the godly. Nothing could be further from the truth! This first part focuses on how God draws near to the radically undeserving.

Do you feel lost and confused?

Brandon was lost. Only a few minutes ago, he had been playing with his older sister; now she was nowhere in sight. His mom was missing too. They had all been shopping, but that quickly got boring for Brandon. He and Teresa had started a game of hide-and-seek among the clothes racks. Teresa hid first and Brandon quickly found her. Then it was his turn. Brandon was a champion hider. Being only two-and-a-half enabled him to stand inside the racks on the lower cross bars so no one could see his legs. Completely hidden by the clothes, he was undetectable.

At first he could hear Teresa though she could neither see nor hear him. Brandon giggled quietly as she came closer toward him and then veered off. As she moved farther and farther away, Brandon heard her voice growing softer. Then it was quiet. Too quiet. Boringly quiet. Brandon decided to liven things up by revealing himself and winning the game. He peeked out, his face full of triumph. Jumping out, he announced, "I win, Terri!" But Teresa didn't scoop him up or tousle his hair. She was gone.

Brandon's triumph turned to puzzlement as he looked around and saw no one he knew. Slowly he walked around the display and still saw neither his sister nor his mother. Then he struck out through the maze of merchandise. Soon, hopelessly confused, he began to panic in earnest. "Mama, Terri! Mama, Terri!" he cried. His legs carried him along though he was blinded with tears. Brandon was desperate. He didn't know where to go or what to do. All he wanted was for his mother and sister to come looking for him. He wanted to be found.

BEING LOST

Have you ever been lost? I don't mean the ten-minutes-on-the-high-way-with-a-map lost. I mean absolutely-no-idea-which-way-to-go lost, where all the points on the compass are equally meaningful and, there-fore, equally useless. In *Bonfire of the Vanities*, Tom Wolfe describes a man who takes a wrong exit in New York City and ends up in a danger-ous section of the Bronx. Wolfe captures this man's progression from cavalier confusion to barely bridled fear to irrational desperation. Have you ever been there? Do you know what it's like to know you need something, know you can't provide it, and only wish someone would come to find you?

For many of us, being lost has nothing to do with geography. Lost is not a place; it is a daily life experience. We can go through the motions of daily life fairly successfully, yet all along we feel as though things are not right. We are deeply dissatisfied with life, yet we have little or no idea what is wrong and certainly no idea how to improve our lot. Thoreau's conclusion that "most men live lives of quiet desperation" describes us fairly well. Existential lostness is a nearly universal experience after humanity's fall.

DESPERATE AND LOST

Zacchaeus was lost.[1] In his hometown, on a road he knew well, he was desperately lost. He just didn't realize how far gone he was.

He wanted to see Jesus, but so did lots of other people. He couldn't get through the crowd, so he climbed a tree for a better look. We might suppose his vantage point was similar to hanging out on a balcony to watch a parade; he was up above the crowd and had a better view. But trees and balconies don't share the same status. Typically, climbing trees is not something that wealthy men of the world engage in. Trees tend to be reserved for children.

My children love to climb trees and I don't blame them. I did too when I was a boy. But an adult in a tree draws attention. If you drive down a street and see kids playing in a tree, you smile and keep going. But if you noticed a grown man up there, you would probably slow down and wonder what was going on.

There's something about post-adolescents in trees that suggests the dangerous (older bodies don't flex or heal as well as younger ones) and

---

[1] Luke 19:1-10.

the ridiculous. Zacchaeus, a wealthy, feared government official, set himself up to be ridiculed for the rest of his life. Embarrassing stories tend to develop a life of their own. Even today Sunday school songs immortalize this man's peculiar behavior! So here's this little man, who probably already had endured his share of insults regarding his height, providing raw material for new, embarrassing stories. Why is he doing this?

It could have been simple curiosity that drove him to go looking for Jesus, but curiosity is not enough to drive someone to such desperate behavior. I have never endangered my reputation for the sake of satisfying simple curiosity. Something else drove Zacchaeus. Despite his wealth, his life was not going well. We're not told what was wrong, but as you consider the lengths he went to, you realize he wanted something more – something that even his wealth couldn't give him. He was dissatisfied with his life and his dissatisfaction drove him to seek out Jesus. To mix metaphors, Zacchaeus was up a tree without a paddle.

Poor Zacchaeus! His money can't give him what he wants so he embarrasses himself to see if Jesus can. Doesn't your heart go out to him as he tries so hard to see the Lord? As with Brandon, you want to scoop him up and help him. But the crowd apparently didn't feel the same way. No one moved aside so the little guy could see. I wonder why?

Zacchaeus was a tax collector. Today, it's difficult for us to imagine what that meant to people then. I dislike paying taxes as much as (or possibly more than) the next guy, but I don't hate the people who work for the IRS. Nor would I try to keep one out of church or away from a public event. But even if I did, I'm still only one person; he could get around me. Here's a case, however, where an entire crowd collectively prevents one man from getting through. They really didn't like him. Whatever he'd done must have been really bad to get that reaction.

And it was. Tax collectors were not just civil servants, they were also professional thieves. Not only did they collect the tax Rome imposed, they imposed additional levies to feather their own nests. Their job gave them an opportunity to rob people using the weight of Roman authority. Zacchaeus stole from his own people. When Luke tells you he was a chief collector, and a rich one, he's making it clear that Zacchaeus had stolen a lot of money from a lot of people.

GREED'S REWARD

Rich people who live at the expense of others end up shrinking their own souls while they squeeze others' pockets. Sadly, the news media regularly reminds us that greed isn't restricted to fiction or ancient history.

Many people seek to better themselves at the expense of others. Can you name "ministers" who beg for money from people on fixed incomes to build lavish mansions for themselves? How about executives who plunder company profits and assets so that they grow wealthy while bankrupting the employee pension funds? Others trade stocks based on insider information – making a killing while your investments take a beating – effectively emptying your bank account into their own. You can do little against such people who knowingly undermine, impoverish, and hurt you.

Zacchaeus was a small man, but his was not a pitiable shortness. Rather, he was monstrous, a parasitic man who grew fat on the blood of others, fully aware that his theft made their lives significantly worse. He idolized money, but instead of getting what he wanted, he harvested the rotten fruit of the crowd's hatred and his own dissatisfaction. He was getting what he had coming to him. Kind of served him right, didn't it?

Yet out of the entire crowd, Jesus singled him out and chose to go to his home. Why? There must have been more deserving people present. Jesus could have had a decent meal without raising questions of conscience. Many in the town were probably eating dry, moldy bread that night because the money Zacchaeus stole from them went to fund Jesus' dinner. Yet Jesus chose to break bread with this odious traitor.

What did Jesus see in the man that drew him – some redeemable trait, some inkling of love for God, or latent drop of humanity? Was that why Jesus moved toward him? If you look for such things in the passage, you'll be disappointed.

Luke 19 notes none of these things as the reason Jesus demanded to eat with him. Many people were seeking Jesus; what made Zacchaeus stand out? Jesus explains his choice simply by saying that he came to seek and to save the lost (v. 10). The quality that drew Jesus to Zacchaeus was the fact that he was a lost man.

In seeking out Zacchaeus, God shows you his heart. So often we talk about what Jesus did or said but ignore his attitude toward us and what drives him. Your God is passionate. He's on a mission. Jesus came to look for those who wander through life dazed and confused, often by their own fault. He searched them out intently, looking beyond those who clamored for his attention to locate those who had no hope. Jesus was not put off by Zacchaeus's despicable sins. He did not recoil from him. Rather, Jesus saw his lostness and found him.

Jesus is the same today. The same grace that moved him to leave heaven and cross time and space to find one pathetic conniver half-hidden in a tree is the same grace that moves him to look for you. He looked for you when you first came to know him and he looks for you even now. Desperate people – lost, confused, frightened – need to know that God searches for them.

That's good news. I don't have anything to commend myself to God to make him notice me. But I know he is compassionate toward people who struggle to make their lives work. That's what I need. I need a God who will come looking for me when I choose making friends with TV characters over spending time with my wife, when I throw myself into work to avoid demanding children, or when I lay around bloated by my lack of self-control, yearning to be entertained. I need a God who comes looking for me when I'm lost. And that's what I have.

Maybe you don't believe that Jesus comes and seeks you out. Sure, you know that it is true theologically. You certainly believe God searches for other people. You even agree that it might be hypothetically possible that he would look for you. But when you're floundering in your sins, feeling desperate, you don't believe he's working diligently to find you. You don't believe that anyone would want to look for you when you're hurting other people, lost in your sin, and don't know what to do.

If that's the case, it's time to fight the fight of faith. Will you allow yourself to believe that Jesus wants to find you right now? That he's looking for you this very moment and won't quit until he finds you? What does the faith battle look like? Often it's a simple acknowledgment: "Jesus, I don't really believe that you want to find me. Please help me believe. Please find me. I want to know that I matter enough to you that you would seek me out when everyone else pushes me away."

JOY ARRIVES

Being found made Zacchaeus a joyful man. Notice that nothing external about his life had changed. He was still a chief tax collector. He had still ruined people's lives. The crowd still hated him . . . he was still short! Yet suddenly he's joyful because Jesus loved him and had entered his life. Jesus alone produced an explosion of joy in him.

Have you lost your joy? Then you've likely forgotten, or little realized, how dreadfully lost you were. Perhaps you've forgotten how wonderful it is for the God of the universe to want to be your Father, Savior, and friend. Sometimes we treat him as the consolation prize: "Well, I don't have a girlfriend, a job I like, or a BMW, but at least I have Jesus." No wonder we have trouble being joyful! Joyless, dried-up people have forgotten where they've come from, which means they've forgotten how Jesus has treated them. Now they take him for granted.

Zacchaeus points the way for joyless people. Spend some time remembering how badly lost you were. Think back to the time before you knew Jesus and how kind he was in searching you out. Think back to your lostness this morning when you criticized your husband, picked a fight with your roommate, or swore at another driver. Then consider how good Jesus is to keep searching for you, knowing he will find you. When you meditate on the two realities of being lost and having a Savior who doesn't quit until he finds you, you can't help but experience joy.

on your own

1 How do you experience being "lost"? What thoughts or feelings describe your experience: "I feel empty inside," "Something is missing," "I don't know where I'm going," "I can't stand myself"? Why do you think you feel lost?

2 What makes it difficult to believe that Jesus comes looking for you? Things you've done? Things you haven't done? Who you are? Spend some time confessing the ways you believe you've disqualified yourself from his search.

3 How many Scripture passages can you remember that show God seeking out his wayward or troubled people until he finds them? Here are a few to get you started: Genesis 28:10-15; Exodus 2:23-25; Judges 6:11-12; 1 Kings 19:1-9; Luke 15:1-7; and Acts 9:1-19. When have you experienced God seeking you? Thank him for being a God who looks for his children.

4 When was the last time you felt joyful? Since true joy is part of the fruit of the Spirit, you can always experience more of it. Welcome joy – ask for joy! – as you meditate on your God's pursuit of you in your lostness.

Do you think God
is out to get you?

Being found produced joy in Zacchaeus. But sometimes being found can be a frightening experience. Our cat, for example, though fairly well socialized into the Smith household, retains her preference for nighttime activities. She hunts for things that come out at night; sometimes she decides she'd like company and tries to rouse one of the children. Since she's not very graceful, her nocturnal activities occasionally wake me up. However, unlike our children, I don't like being disturbed by a playful pet. My (ungodly) response to such interruptions is to try to make her think twice about doing it again.

The other night I awoke to an odd noise. It was the cat again, scrabbling at the carpet under my daughter's bed. Arming myself with a pole, I successfully dislodged the nuisance (much to my daughter's bemusement, who pretended to be asleep). But at 5:00 A.M., I was infuriated, not bemused, so after getting the cat out of my daughter's room, I continued my pursuit. Having been on the receiving end of the hunt before, the cat bolted down the stairs searching for a place to hide.

The chase began in earnest as I closed potential exit doors behind me, turned on lights, and peered under furniture. The cat ran vainly from closed door to lighted room, with me hot on her trail. Cats are incredibly fast, but I was incredibly – comically – determined.

In full sprint, but sensing her rapidly diminishing options, the poor creature suddenly stopped, looked at me, and mewed plaintively, her anguish obvious in posture and voice. At that moment, chastened by her distress, I allowed her to slink away unmolested.

Clearly, if you are a restless cat in the middle of the night, I am a dangerous person to have come looking for you. You don't want me to find you. But if you are a rebellious human, God is a very safe person to have search for you. You want him to find you because he will not leave you frightened or dismayed.

A KIND FINDER

Adam and Eve didn't expect God to be safe when they rebelled against him.[1] They knew what he sounded like when he came walking in the cool of the day, and when they heard him, they went the other way. Not anticipating a positive meeting, they attempted to hide. Notice how quickly these people, who had never experienced a negative moment with their Creator, expected an unpleasant encounter. Sin strikes quickly and dramatically at relationships!

Unfortunately, the effect of sin on relationships is all too common an experience for people who sin against us. We can hardly blame people for wanting to run and hide when they're in the wrong. Think about the ways you react when your children refuse to get ready for bed, or when your husband embarrasses you, or your employee misses a deadline.

Some believe it's their right to pour out their anger when another sins against them. "After all I've done for you, this is how you treat me? This is how you repay me?!" Others run out of breath listing all the ways the person has hurt them. Others resort to ridicule, aiming to humiliate the person in front of people close to him or her. There is almost no end to the crushing ways we handle each other's failings. We provide powerful incentives for others to run and hide rather than confess what they have done wrong.

But God is different. He doesn't swoop down on Adam and Eve and start demanding, "What were you thinking?!" He doesn't berate, badger, and interrogate them. Nor does he hold himself aloof, waiting for them to make the first move. Instead, he comes to them. They know they have ruined everything, and they have no idea how to make things right. They're not even sure they can. God knows they're afraid, and so he comes to them.

It's bad enough confronting someone when he or she has wronged you. It feels unfair. You think, *Why should I confront you? You wronged me; you should take the first step to make this right.* It's even worse when you have to go looking for the person. Do you enjoy chasing your child upstairs to confront her for yelling that she hates you – a child who owes her life, breath, and CD collection to your faithful care? You don't

---

[1] Gen. 3:1-24.

want to pursue people who sin against you, but most of the time you will have to. Adam and Eve didn't pursue God, so he pursued them.

Why? If God had had evil intentions, wanting to destroy them or make them suffer, then he could have just thrown lightening bolts. *Voilà* – problem solved! When he goes looking for them, you realize that he must have redemptive goals in mind.

Given the pervasive destruction caused by their rebellion, if there ever was a time or place for tracking someone down and letting him have it, this is that time and God is that one person who could justifiably do so! But when you read this passage for the first time, cringing for our eldest parents' sake, wondering what God might do, you find that he does something extraordinarily mundane. He asks a question.

Now I might ask a question too, but it would have an edge to it and be rhetorical. "What do you think you are doing?! You've wrapped *my* fig leaves around you and hid yourself in *my* bushes hoping that I won't see you? This is the kind of wisdom you hoped to get from eating the fruit?" Instead, God asks an honest question that allows them to respond without being boxed in.

Adam and Eve have just ruined all of creation, yet God wants to talk with them. That should amaze you. Here is a God they could have come to with the mess they made. They didn't have to hide from him. And look at his question: "Where are you?" Where are you?! I thought God knew everything! Why is he asking geography questions? As you ponder his question, you realize he doesn't need the answer. That means he's not asking for his benefit . . . he's asking for Adam's.

God doesn't need the interaction. Adam needs the experience of answering the question. Adam needs the responsibility of owning what he has done and God gives him an opportunity to do so without terrorizing him. God follows up the first question with another and, even though Adam and Eve attempt to shift the blame away from themselves, God promises to send them someone who will deliver them from what they have done. Better than allowing them to shift the blame, God himself will take the punishment they deserve.

Even after pronouncing the consequences of their actions – toil and pain – God remains concerned for their welfare. He covers their nakedness and eases their embarrassment. He does not hold a grudge. But he realizes that if they take hold of the Tree of Life, which would give them eternal life, in their current condition, they will live forever in the horrible state of sin in which they are mired.

So, in mercy, God sends them out of Eden.[2] I hate the sin that regularly trips me up this side of heaven. I hate the ways I so easily dishonor Christ and hurt those around me. But what would it be like to live like that forever? I have hope that a day is coming when I will be completely free from a critical spirit, mixed motives, manipulating, double-dealing, and gossiping. Life would be unbearable if there were no hope of being free of those sins. God does not want his creatures' present hopelessness and alienation to be permanent. His concern for their welfare moves him to send them out of the garden and guard against their return. Now there is hope for future release from sin.

Sin produced fear in Adam and Eve. It drove them into hiding. But God's response went deeper than their fear. He searched for them, desiring to do them good. Yes, they suffered consequences for their actions, but those consequences were from a God who had their best interests at heart.

He is the same God today. He comes looking for you when you sin and fail. More than that, he is a God you want to come looking for you. You know that when he finds you he will make things better. True, he knows you're in trouble; you may have put yourself in danger. But he does not seek to ruin you. He seeks to rescue you. There will be consequences, but there will be goodness in those consequences. How could you be frightened when he comes looking for you? Instead, you are really glad he is seeking you out. It moves you to thankful worship.

What's your favorite way to hide? Some people distract themselves with busy schedules, toys, and amusement. They experience guilt of the unproductive kind – the kind that doesn't drive them to Christ – so they allow it to dull their awareness of their need to run to God. It feels easier.

Other people hang onto a disastrous failure from years past; it haunts them every time they try to pray. Others are snowed under by an avalanche of sins that drives them from God's presence by its sheer volume. Such people rightly see the scope of their failure and their inability to make it go away. They rightly believe in God's holiness, justice, and wrath; but, wrongly, that is all they see of God.

Underneath each way you hide from God lies your belief that God will not receive you or that God intends to harm you. You believe that your sin so separates you from God that no bridge could ever reconnect you. You rightly believe in God's holiness, justice, and wrath, but not as strongly in his goodness. Adam and Eve had the same reaction. When

---

[2] Gen. 3:22-24.

they faced God, however, they learned that his mercy and kindness are as deep as his justice and anger. What holds you back from encountering this God?

The Bible does talk about people who should be terrified to have God look for them: those who ignore him, those who test him by refusing his authority, and those who are hypocrites. He warns such people that the only thing awaiting them is judgment and wrath. God is very clear that he will be severe with them. Ironically, those are the very people who tend to be deaf to his warnings!

Perhaps this is one way of determining if you should be scared of having God come look for you. If his warnings have no effect on you, you probably should be scared to death! But if God's words are important to you, if you desire to obey him and are grieved at failing him, you can come to him confidently when you sin. He is looking for you with mercy on his mind.

1   How do you run and hide from God? Do you work or play harder to avoid dealing with Jesus? Do you treat your sin too lightly (not giving it enough weight in light of God's holiness) or too heavily (so that it out-weighs God's mercy)?

2   What holds you back from running to Christ when you sin? Make a list of the lies you believe in those moments. What does this list tell you about what you really think of God and his character? How does your list slander the good intentions of his heart?

3   Think back over your experiences with God. How has he proven in the past that he pursues you to do you good? You'd be well served by making a list of the times he has not let you get away with something or has run to care for you when you've rebelled. Such a list counteracts the lie list of Question 2.

4   Now it's time to practice running to him instead of from him. Hiding from him is an act of unbelief that assumes he hates you. Hiding is sin; yet even as you silently slander his character, God moves toward you to rescue you. So turn now; run to him to deal with your unbelief. Spend some time in prayer confessing how you've run from him, falsely believing that he'd treat you badly. Ask him to give you faith to believe that he has good intentions when he pursues you. Thank him for being better than you thought and treating you more kindly than you deserve.

Do you doubt that Jesus would ever want to be your friend?

I trust my boss. He likes me. He smiles when I walk into his office, puts aside his projects, and tries hard to get me what I need. I bring some positive things to the table as well. I get things done, do them well, and, in general, contribute more resources than I consume. You might be tempted to conclude that my confidence in my boss's regard for me is based on how well I do my job. But our relationship extends beyond the ways I've been helpful to him.

The first time we met, he was teaching a course I was taking. For some inexplicable reason, he asked for feedback on how the class had gone. Feedback from seminary students? That's always a dangerous thing to ask for, especially from arrogant, inexperienced hotheads like me! Although the comments I offered were not overtly insulting, they were pointed and critical of his teaching style. "Unwise" was how my wife described them.

His response, however, was not to get angry and lash out. Nor did he wilt and try to appease me. Instead, he invited me to lunch to discuss my concerns. We had a reasoned and amiable conversation in which we sought to understand each other better. I learned to appreciate what he was doing in class and I think he got a better picture of what I was trying to say.

I learned something much more valuable that afternoon than how to get along with others or teach a class. I saw a man who could handle a brash young upstart without giving in or being threatened. His goodness evidenced itself in seeking to bridge the gap between us. That lunch gave me reason to trust him and that trust remains to this day. I know that he doesn't treat me the way he does just because I make his life easier – there are plenty of times when I don't! He treats me well because it's part of his nature; that's why I have learned to trust him. His response to intemperate comments revealed the kind of man he is and he made a better relationship possible. Ironically, you most clearly see another person's commitment to relationships when you are at your worst. And that's true of God as well. His commitment to us shone clearly as he handled one of humanity's worst moments.

GOD IS KIND TO THE UNDESERVING

We learn in Romans 1 that God created the universe to display his glory, to make visible his invisible qualities – his eternal power and divine nature.[1] This means that what you see in nature tells you something about him. When you look at a tree's countless leaves, you're meant to understand something about God's infinity, his beauty, his creativity, and his abundant life. And then you are meant to bow in worship as you imagine what God conveys to you through an entire forest!

That means when you see creation unfold in Genesis 1, you are witnessing the unfolding of his glory. God says, "Let there be light," and the angels gasp, not just because they see light, but because the existence of light reveals God more clearly. God separates the waters and the gasps grow louder as more of their Maker is revealed. As the process continues, more of God's glory unfolds. At each successive stage, the angels see more and more of their God, and they praise him with greater knowledge and insight. And then, at the pinnacle of creation, to reveal himself most clearly and brightly, God makes humans in his image. The angels simply marvel. Here, among all the wonders and majesty of the universe, stand the best reflection of who and what God is. Here was glory so real, so tangible, that the little, inconsequential planet floating in the heavens blazed like a beacon across the universe, proclaiming not humanity's worth and value, but the Holy Creator's.

And then these wonderful images – whose every thought, action, and breath shout "Here's who God is!" – rebel against him. They no longer proclaim the Great Creator. Now they proclaim the Great Deceiver. In rejecting their lofty, highborn state, they send a loud obscenity rolling across the heavens. They take the bright light that the world was and, in an instant, snuff it out.

And so do you. When you hurl insults at your wife, refuse to listen to your parents, or provoke your children, you rebel against your God.

---

[1] Rom. 1:19-20.

When you deceive your boss about when your project will be done, take six inches of your neighbor's yard for your garden, or fail to report all of your income to the IRS, you proclaim the Great Deceiver. When you sow division in your church, fantasize about another woman's husband, or manhandle your kids, your obscenities echo across the heavens. You and I regularly shatter the glory God intended to shine from this planet. And in the same moment, we shatter any hope of relationship with such a glorious person.

Once Adam and Eve had rebelled, the stage was set for God to enter and pronounce his judgment.[2] Do you remember the penalty for rebellion? "When you eat of it [the fruit], you will surely die."[3] Adam and Eve deserved instant annihilation, but they weren't immediately destroyed. The fact that they were still alive to hear the curses is an indication of what? Of grace. Any time you get less horror than you deserve, you are getting grace. Adam and Eve deserved the penalty of hell without delay, just like the fallen angels. But they didn't get it.

God tells Adam that by the sweat of his brow he will eat.[4] Wait a minute! This animated dust has utterly defiled the image of God, and God not only lets him live but implicitly promises that he will continue to feed him. We tend to focus on the toil and sweat part and forget that God's promise of ongoing nourishment is not a right that Adam naturally had. It was God's kind provision even before Adam and Eve rebelled, but now it is far more than kind. It is grace.

When we come to Eve, we all focus on the pain of childbirth.[5] But have you stopped to consider what it means that women are still able to bear children? To modern ears this will sound strange, so I ask your indulgence, but from the perspective of the author of Genesis, the primary way woman helps man is by giving birth. In so doing, she continues the human race in its mission of proclaiming the glory of the invisible God to the universe. This is why it is so dreadful to Old Testament women like Sarah, Rebekah, Rachel, and Leah when they were unable to bear children. God does not take this ability away from Eve. Her primary purpose and meaning in life, at least from the perspective of Genesis, remains hers. For Adam, work becomes labor, but he is still permitted meaningful employment in ruling the earth. What else can you call ongoing meaning and purpose, but grace?

---

2 Gen. 3:14-19.
3 Gen. 2:17.
4 Gen. 3:17-19.
5 Gen. 3:16.

Perhaps, however, God's greatest mercy to humanity is revealed in his curse of the Serpent. Remember that we, his images, are not simple signposts that point to the glory of God. In God's mind, we are his companions. God wants to relate to his creatures.

This is an astounding thing. It requires a sin-soaked heart and mind to make it dull and boring. God wants to be friends with you. He does not create human servants to do his dirty work or feed some twisted craving. He creates people in his own likeness and treats them like his children. He provides for them, visits them, and speaks to them. He longs for relationship. Rebellion shatters his glory and it also breaks this special relationship.

And to this rejection, which no human tale of unrequited love can equal, God responds with grace. Speaking to the Serpent, God says, "And I will put enmity between you and the woman, and between your offspring and hers; he will crush your head, and you will strike his heel."[6] In cursing the Serpent, God, in effect, says to his wayward offspring, "You chose to build an alliance against me, but I love you too much to let it stand. You are my children and you may not continue in rebellion against me. I'm stepping in for your good. I won't let you be friends with Satan!"

Wow! A God who won't let you have what will surely destroy you. A God who uses his power to act in your best interests. Here again – in the curses, no less – you see a gracious God. Confronted with treasonous disloyalty, he commits himself to rebuilding relationships with his people.

RECONCILIATION THROUGH THE AGES

And that is just a start. As you make your way through the Scriptures, you see God moving closer and closer to his people. Early on he draws near in the theophanies, the strange appearances of God in the Old Testament, where he speaks with individuals like Abraham, Jacob, Moses, and Joshua.[7] It must have been wonderful to actually meet with God, but those times were sporadic. You couldn't initiate one of those meetings; they happened without warning. He usually came disguised – wandering traveler, angel, champion wrestler – so that the human participants didn't always seem to know who they were talking with right away.

God moved beyond theophanies to be closer to his children by instituting the Tabernacle. This allowed the relationship to be much more

---

[6] Gen. 3:15.
[7] Gen. 18:1-5; Gen. 32:24-30; Ex. 3:2-4:17; Josh. 5:13-15; Judg. 6:11-14.

consistent as he lived permanently among his people.[8] All of Israel knew where he could be found at all times, although the location kept moving, making him hard for an outsider to find. However, God had to hide himself behind the curtain in the Holy of Holies to protect his people from being destroyed by his holiness, which was offended by their sinfulness.[9] So he was among his people, but behind a barrier that could only be crossed once a year by the high priest.

God's reconciling relationship with his people took another step forward when he authorized the Temple.[10] Now his location was fixed in one place so that all nations could come to Jerusalem to find him.[11] Unfortunately, once they got there, he was still hidden behind the veil.

And then came Jesus. Incredibly, God stepped out from behind the curtain. In his desire to restore the relationship between himself and his images, he came to them in a human body. John tells us that Jesus "tabernacled" among us – literally, he "pitched his tent."[12] God was no longer hidden. If you saw Christ, you saw the Father. There was now direct contact between God and humanity again. You could touch him and talk with him, though he could only be in one place at a time.

After atoning for our unholiness and returning to heaven, Jesus broke all geographical and temporal boundaries by pouring out his Holy Spirit. Through the Spirit he was no longer shrouded or restricted to one location. We can enjoy direct communication with God anywhere, all the time. As if that were not enough, we look forward to a future we barely understand; a time when we will be interconnected with each other, creating a place where God will choose to live among us.[13]

In short, as his plan unfolds, God comes nearer and nearer to his people. His relational presence becomes more personally intense even while it expands geographically to cover the globe. He restores relationships that have been twisted and destroyed, spreading his image across the earth so that it shines more and more brightly with his glory, as he originally intended.

Our first parents' rebellion should have ended any chance of knowing God (as should your rebellion and mine). But God uses his power to bring

---

8 Ex. 29:44-46; Ex. 40:34-38.
9 Ex. 26:31-35; Lev. 16:1-2; Heb. 9:1-10.
10 1 Kings 6:1-13; 2 Chron. 5:1-14.
11 1 Kings 8:27-30, 41-43.
12 John 1:14. The Greek verb, **skhnów**, meaning to live or dwell, means a tent or tabernacle in its noun form.
13 1 Peter 2:4-5.

blessing in the midst of cursing. We humans bring sin, rebellion, death, and separation to the equation. But God brings forgiveness, reconciliation, life, and restoration. He brings grace that makes friends of his enemies. A God who handles sin and rebellion this way is a God I can trust when I sin and rebel.

God is not merely kind to people who don't deserve it. He does more than simply help me when I'm struggling and then send me on my way. Instead he pursues me to restore our relationship – the most precious and beautiful thing in the universe – and to defeat my destructive rebellion. Seeing the goal of God's kindness at humanity's worst moment increases my trust in him. Yes, there are consequences to my failings, but they are nowhere near what I deserve. Our God keeps pursuing us for relationship, doing what must be done to ensure that it happens.

Once again the faith question lies right on the surface: Do you believe it? Do you believe that God wants to be your friend? Perhaps you believe that God searches diligently for you. You can even muster up the faith to believe that he's doing so for your good. But when you think about all the glorious creatures in the universe and all the truly interesting people who have something to offer, you can't quite believe that God thinks you're especially worth knowing. Sure, you reason, he had to restore relationship with Adam and Eve so that the human race continued, but there doesn't seem to be much lost if he doesn't connect with me. Or maybe you think that the things you have done disqualify you from experiencing his merciful intimacy.

You wouldn't be the first to believe those lies. They're the same ones Satan has told for years: that God doesn't truly love his children or really want to know them. There's just enough reasonableness in those thoughts to make them plausible. On one level, it is crazy to believe that the Creator would want anything to do with you or me. I mean, what's in it for him? But it is God himself who says that he wants us, and he backs his words with his actions. These actions show you his heart for you personally. He will do – and has done – literally anything to get you back.

Now it's your turn. Do you believe him even after you've failed him? More importantly, do you want the friendship with him that he desires?

on your own

1 How much does God's desire to befriend you color your thoughts of him? Do you believe him? What makes you think he isn't serious?

2 God has spent history moving closer to his people. Reflect on your own life: are you in sync with the rhythm of the universe by desiring to move closer to him? Or has your relationship stalled? Is knowing him less interesting than it once was? What has replaced your desire to draw closer to him?

3 Jesus wants to build a relationship with you, yet sometimes Christian methods of knowing God can hinder this goal. Have you ever had devotional times because you'd feel guilty if you didn't? Or studied your Bible so that you would feel better about yourself? What other religious motivations can hinder the relationship? Ask him to forgive you for doing things that look good but ultimately separate you from him.

4 We all need to practice seeing God's ongoing graciousness in our lives, especially when only the curses seem evident. Think about your past week or the last serious hard time you had. In what concrete ways did God extend his kindness to you? Talk with him about his kindness and how thankful you are to him.

Do you worry that you'll wear out God's patience?

What does faith look like when it reaches back to this wonderful, seeking God? If you believe the children's versions of Bible stories, being faithful is the same as being perfect. The standard story formula involves a spotless hero who consistently loves God, tries hard, never messes up, and is rewarded for his virtue. Rarely are children presented with a person who is anything less than perfectly wholesome.

That's understandable when you consider how Americans write their own life histories. What would you like to read in your biography? You'd want to be cast in the best light possible. You'd like the author to focus on your achievements and not question your character. Maybe you'd allow a small question, so that readers would know you're human, but it would need to be small enough not to tarnish the lustrous shine on the rest of your life.

You wouldn't mind a little omission here, a little embellishment there. And you certainly would prefer to exclude the times you waffled on important decisions, made errors in judgments, and were simply stupid. In short, you would prefer your story be told by someone other than God! When God tells our story, there is full disclosure. We see it in the way the Bible talks about Abraham.

Big Sinners

In Genesis 12, Abraham, the man of faith, leaves Canaan, his promised land, as soon as God gives it to him. When a famine occurs, he goes to Egypt. This might not seem earth-shaking, but that is because you're not part of the book's original audience. Those first readers and hearers had been slaves in Egypt; they knew it as a place of death. When we're told that Abraham voluntarily chose to go there, it foreshadows trouble. It's like watching a movie when the heroine walks up a dark stairway toward a closed door. You clutch your seat, silently screaming, Don't go in there! In Genesis you're meant to understand that Abraham's relocation was a bad move on his part, quite possibly even a faithless one in light of what God just promised him.

While in Egypt, Abraham lies about his wife, calling her his sister because he is afraid that someone might kill him to have her for himself. As a result, Sarah is absorbed into Pharaoh's harem![1] True, God rescues her by sending disease on Pharaoh's household, but what a risk Abraham took! How did Abraham and Sarah resume their life together after this experience and what it revealed about Abraham's character and his commitment to his wife? God clearly doesn't protect Abraham's reputation by telling us only the good things about him.

As if one self-serving betrayal were not enough, Abraham later repeats the same ruse with similar results.[2] And, following in his father's footsteps, Isaac employs the same dodge years later[3] with nearly the same disastrous outcome for *his* wife. Neither father of the faith appears terribly faithful when it comes to trusting God for his life – or his wife. Part of the peculiar irony of these three accounts is that the pagan kings act with greater reverence for God than do Abraham or Isaac.

Abraham is hardly a role model when it comes to his son Ishmael either. Even though it was culturally acceptable, Abraham strained his family by fathering Ishmael with Sarah's maidservant Hagar. It was a faithless attempt to fulfill God's promise that he would be the father of many through Sarah.[4] On top of that, he relinquished responsibility for the ensuing disharmony between the women and allowed Sarah to drive Hagar away.[5]

If this were your family, you wouldn't want other people to know about these events. Instead of parading the family skeletons for other people to inspect, you'd leave them safely locked in forgotten closets. Don't you find it odd that God chooses to bring such matters to our attention?

Please remember that Abraham is hardly the worst person in Genesis. His nephew Lot craves the good life and ends up destroying his family. Jacob deceives and manipulates his way through life. And, apart from the sheer number of his children, he does not distinguish himself as a family man. The in-fighting between Leah and Rachel soon escalates

---

[1] Gen. 12:10-20.
[2] Gen. 20.
[3] Gen. 26:1-11.
[4] Gen. 17:15-21.
[5] Gen. 16:5-6.

to their children's plot to murder their own sibling.[6] They stop short, but only because it's more profitable to sell him as a slave. They then agree to tell their father that Joseph is dead. Perversely, they keep the lie alive for years even though it is slowly killing Jacob.

As you consider this soap opera, remember that God promised that all nations would be blessed through this family. Blessed?! This is not a family you want living next door, much less blessing you. When I look at these men, the mess I make in my own family suddenly doesn't seem so bad. And as I keep reading, the family history only gets worse.

Judah, one of Jacob's sons, impregnates his daughter-in-law, mistaking her for a prostitute.[7] I still can't decide what is most appalling in that story. Is it Judah's ignoring his obligation to provide for Tamar by refusing to marry her to his son? Should we be primarily offended that he hires a prostitute . . . or scandalized that he sleeps with his daughter-in-law?[8] Please don't forget that Jesus is a descendent of this unseemly union! Is this the bloodline you would advertise for your King, for your only Son, whom you love?

Or consider Jacob's sons Levi and Simeon, who scheme to murder the Shechemites, the majority of whom were innocent of any crime against Jacob's family.[9] They loot the city and carry off all the wealth and the women and children. (What were they going to do with them?) Would you choose Levi's descendents to be the priestly clan? These are not the kind of people you would ask to lead worship or staff the children's Sunday school.

BIGGER GOD

In short, Genesis is a book about big sins, sins that many of us are confident we'd never commit. Can you imagine giving your wife to another? Plotting to murder your brother or actually murdering a village? These are shocking sins from which you pull back and smugly say, "I'd *never* do *anything* like *that*!"

That is, you could feel comfortable as long as you only looked at their specific sins and ignored the similarities you share with them. How about the time when, out of fear of what the bully might do, you betrayed a close friend on the playground . . . or in the office cafeteria? Or the time when you ignored the chaos your teenage son brought into your home? You hoped he would just grow up and the problem would

---

[6] Gen. 37:12-35.
[7] Gen. 38:12-19.
[8] Lev. 20:12.
[9] Gen. 34:13-31.

go away – only to find his chaos spiraling out of control, ending in heartbreak you could have avoided. How about when you took advantage of your close friend and wound up with her promotion, her raise, or her boyfriend? Or when your passions overcame your principles, turning your life upside down?

The primary difference between the patriarchs and me may simply be that my skeletons are known to relatively few people while theirs are exhibited across the pages of Scripture. If you are honest, you know you are more like the people you meet in Genesis than you'd like your friends to know. The vivid sins of others may lessen the sting of your own dark secrets, but it never removes or undoes them. You still have the feeling of embarrassment and the hope that no one will ever find out. So do I. We know the desire to compare ourselves to others to make ourselves feel better. But deep down, most of us know that we have not lived what we said we believed. So how do we dare reach out to God with such pitiful, raggedy faith?

Have you ever wondered, *Have I made mistakes so big that the promises of God just can't hold for me any longer? Have I so sinned against God that he's fed up, and I'm going to have to settle for Plan B for the rest of my life? Did I marry the wrong person, buy the wrong house, take the wrong job? Have I wasted my life by pursuing the wrong things for too long?*

If you are haunted by such questions, focus on God's response to his people's multiple failures. He gives Isaac, the child of promise, to Abraham despite Abraham's faithlessness. He remains faithful to Isaac, giving him offspring to continue the promise. God never abandons Jacob and ultimately changes his name to Israel; the "one who deceives" becomes "one who struggles with God and overcomes."[10] He sent Joseph to Egypt ahead of his murderous brothers to provide for them during a famine that would have killed them all and ended the promise.[11] Despite all their failures, God never gave up on the first families he chose. He remained faithful despite their faithlessness.

This reality is very helpful if your sin leaves you wondering, *Have I worn God out? What if he doesn't really want to bother with me anymore?* Genesis doesn't tell stories of perfect people who are blessed for their goodness. They're just as much a mess as most of us. That realization helps you grasp why God exposes all of the sordid things his people do. He does

---

[10] Gen. 35:10.
[11] Gen. 50:20.

it to give you hope. He is not only the author of their faith but the finisher as well. He overwrites their failings . . . and overwrites yours as well.

The golden thread running through Genesis does not belong to any faith-filled, loyal human. It belongs to our fiercely faithful God, who towers benevolently above the mess of his people's lives. Instead of being awed by unattainable ideals of human virtue, you are supposed to see beyond the flawed people in the foreground to a great, big, gracious God behind them, a God who continues to reconcile and redeem. Genesis shows you recurring failures who aren't destroyed! Instead, God befriends them, hangs in there with them, and redeems their lives, creating a family for himself, a family of faith.

FAITH AMID FAILURE

As Hebrews 11 points out, you are to imitate these people's faith. But please remember, it is a faith expressed in the context of many failures. Real faith does not come from having your act together, never making any mistakes or wrong choices. Rather, real faith is lived within the context of being a deeply flawed person.

Romanticized versions of biblical heroes can keep us from connecting with Christ. Can we be confident that God will help us if we are repeatedly taught that God makes life work out well for people who are good? Or is it more likely that we will try first to make ourselves good and then ask for help – or not ask at all, because we are too ashamed? We make more of these saints than they are and then wonder why we cannot relate to them and their faith!

Recognizing that our spiritual forerunners were deeply flawed does not mean that you can get comfortable with your failings. God still expects you to obey him. Instead, you lose your fear of acknowledging your failings. This allows you to develop greater confidence in the love God has for you despite your lack of faith.

Stanton lived with secret lust and immorality for decades. He needed to talk honestly about it with other people, but it was much more important for him to be honest with Christ. One day, while trying to read his Bible, he realized that he was far more interested in immoral sex than he was in Jesus. That's an awful situation to be in! You're trying to have devotions and realize you'd rather be sinning! In the past, this temptation would have led him to close his Bible and run from God, or hypocritically pray, "I want to give this sin up" without actually meaning it.

This time was different. He chose to be honest with Jesus. He began praying and asking for help as he wrestled back and forth, honestly confessing, "I don't want to give this up" and desperately pleading, "I want this out of my life." He acknowledged to Jesus the problem in all its ugliness – not just the attraction of immorality but also his unwillingness to let it go. It was not a fun time. He did not experience a tremendous breakthrough that shattered sin in his life. But he did experience a deeper relationship with Jesus that changed him.

Instead of giving in to his lifelong pursuit of doing what was easy, he faced the issue and brought it to his Lord. It felt like walking uphill on a gravel pile, but he was gaining spiritual traction in his life rather than simply sliding down the stones. He learned to turn to Christ in a moment of sin instead of covering himself and hiding. He learned to believe a little bit more that Christ would receive and restore him. He learned to be faithful in the middle of failure.

LONGING FOR MORE

Recognizing the patriarchs' failings causes you to look forward to Christ. When you read the Old Testament, you start looking for the One who will finally get it all completely right – the one Genesis 3 says will crush the Serpent's head. You keep looking for him and you keep being disappointed. And you should be.

Don't you feel your heart sink when Moses angrily strikes the rock and you realize he can't complete the job God gave him?[12] He is not the one. Don't you burn with righteous anger when David commits adultery and then murders to hide it?[13] Although he was a man after God's own heart, he was also a man whose heart ran after many ungodly things. He is not the one. Do you gasp with regret when you read about Solomon's life? He was devoted to God for twenty years but then loved many foreign women who turned his heart after other gods, weakening his devotion to the Lord his God.[14] That should be hugely disappointing! You're not supposed to remain unmoved when you read about a saint who recklessly pursues idolatry.

Let the stories move you. Let yourself long that much more for Christ. That's God's point in telling them the way he does. You must realize that, like you, these people had no righteousness in themselves. None of them were the Messiah and none of them could live a godly life apart

---

[12] Num. 20:9-12.
[13] 2 Sam. 11.
[14] 1 Kings 11:1-6.

from him. Part of the buildup of the Old Testament is a greater longing for the promised One who is yet to come.

Those two things – seeing the Bible characters' imperfections coupled with a greater longing for Christ – will guard you from looking for perfection in yourself. Instead, your gratefulness to God and your desire to be with him will grow. You will recognize how infinitely great and good he is and you will want to know him that much more.

When I focus on who God is and what he's doing, it changes how I live. If I believe that God is at work despite how badly I have failed, I begin to be more concerned with what he is doing now. I worry less about my own sins and failures, though I do not take them lightly. Remembering and believing God's plan gives me hope. I can grab hold of life and live faithfully today rather than stay paralyzed by yesterday's failures.

God pursues you for relationship through multiple instances of faithlessness. He is in the relationship for the long haul. And because he knows you cannot sustain your end of the relationship, he bases it on his faithfulness, not yours. He knows what he's getting into and he's up for the challenge! He remains faithful when you are faithless. Are you ready to look beyond your faithlessness and trust his faithfulness? Are you ready to let go of your dreams of being perfect and rest instead in his perfect pursuit and provision for you?

on your own

1   What skeletons are you afraid others might discover if they knew more
    about you? How has your desire to keep them hidden "protected" you
    from growing in confidence in Christ's love for you?

2   How do such embarrassments tempt you to believe that God's promises
    and plans for his people don't include you? Confess to him that you don't
    believe he can remain faithful when you haven't.

3   Are you tempted to equate faithful living with perfect living? Faithfulness
    and holiness feed each other; both are part of a healthy Christian life. But
    sometimes we can become so focused on the goal of a holy life that the
    pursuit of sinless perfection replaces a desire to know Christ. Ask yourself
    if that might be true of you. Here's a question that has challenged me on
    numerous occasions: Would being perfect in heaven be enough for you if
    Jesus weren't there?

4   Be honest with Christ about your fearfulness, lack of faith, and desire to
    make up for your own shortcomings. This is an area where you need wise
    friends to help you. Consider opening up some of your dark closets to a
    close friend, small group leader, or pastor.

Do you feel as if Jesus has to put up with you (and wishes he didn't)?

O kay, so God is in it for my good and he is in it for the long haul. But what's his attitude? Is he just putting up with me while he's building this relationship? Has he wearily resigned himself to keeping rash promises he wishes he hadn't made? How can I know how he feels about me? You know how he feels by watching the way he responds to his people. Just as your heart expresses itself through your actions, so does God's.

Several years ago I was reading Ephesians when I was struck by how special people are. Paul describes how God suddenly makes spiritually dead people alive, lifts them into heaven, seats them next to himself, and pours out on them the riches of his grace – for all eternity![1] I thought, *Wow! How much more special can you get?* Paul continues at length about all the privileges we will enjoy. If gifts are any indication of how much you value someone, then God truly values his people. It was a transforming moment for me when I realized that people really matter to Christ.

When I shared this insight with a friend, he wondered, in his inimitable, understated way, if those passages actually showed more of the special-ness of Christ. At the time I didn't really understand what he meant: I was too focused on the status God had given to his people. I didn't see that the One who did those wonderful things for broken, sinful, dead people had to be *really* special. In other words, the gifts God gives reveal how extraordinary *he* is. Lavishing them on undeserving humans underlines *his* goodness.

Ephesians allows you to see how wonderful God is by describing what he does. That's true of the entire Bible. It tells many stories about people, but within those stories you watch a marvelous Redeemer willingly and gladly redeem. Beyond showing you what God does, these stories let you glimpse his heart. The story of Lot comforts me on this score.[2]

---

[1] Eph. 2:1-10.
[2] Gen. 12:4; 13:1-13.

Riches to Rags

Who is Lot – apart from being another serious contender for the "Most Ruined Life" award? To begin with, he has the right bloodline. If you want to survive all eternity, you need to be part of God's family, which, from the standpoint of Genesis, means you have to be connected to Abraham. Lot has this going for him. Lot also demonstrates faith when he journeys with his uncle Abraham to the land God would show him. On top of that, Lot is prosperous. He has been blessed with so much stuff that he and Abraham cannot manage it all within the same geographical area. Again, within the worldview of Genesis, this is to experience the blessing of God. Lot is well connected. He acted in faith and is blessed by God. It's hard to have a better start than that.

Lot's trajectory, however, follows that of an earth-bound missile as he moves away from his uncle toward Sodom and Gomorrah. Having once owned flocks and herds that rivaled Abraham's, he eventually fled Sodom and Gomorrah without a single possession.[3] At one time he enjoyed the security of his uncle's army (which defeated an enemy that five kings together could not).[4] Lot went from that shelter to live in a prosperous city. From there, he fled to a small town and hid in a cave.[5] Worse yet, he exchanged a position of honor in a God-fearing community for the respect of the odious Sodomites.[6] He completed his downward spiral by living with incestuous daughters and fathering his own grandsons.[7]

Lot is tempted and charmed by the attractions of the world. When he pursued them instead of the promises of God, he wound up ruining his family. His wife's longings destroyed her and his daughters took their sexual corruption with them. When he made his home in Sodom, Sodom made its home in his family. Lot reached for it all and ended up with nothing.

And that is so easy to do! No one sets out to become a pathological liar so that, by the time she's fifty-three, everyone doubts every word she says. No one plans to turn into a glutton who wheezes whenever he climbs the stairs or has to squeeze behind his car's steering wheel. No one seeks to end up miserly, hypersensitive, or anxious. People become what they are by making small choices, one after another, over periods of time.

Lot did not wake up one day and say to himself, *I think I'd like to lose everything I value and live among radically depraved people who*

---

3 Gen. 19:16.
4 Gen. 14:8-16.
5 Gen. 19:18-21, 30.
6 Gen. 19:1.
7 Gen. 19:31-38.

will influence my daughters to be immoral. Now, what's the best way to make that happen? But those were the consequences he set in motion by making small, self-serving choices. He chose the best-looking land for his own, moved his tent nearer to the big city, relocated within it and became a leading citizen who sat in the gate. Little by little, Lot grew more and more comfortable with people who should have made him feel more and more disturbed. Each step along the way was easy because it was small. But each step moved him farther from his God, and he paid a dreadful price.

GOD, WHO IS RICH IN MERCY

What do you learn from this? On the surface, Lot's life is a warning about not following the lust of the eyes, a powerful case study in the danger of walking away from God's people to pursue the so-called good life. But there is so much more to this story than warnings about temptation, which assume that Lot is the story's star attraction. When you realize that the primary purpose of the Bible is to reveal God – and ultimately to reveal Christ – the story becomes a great deal richer.

God shows his kindness to Lot by rescuing him not once, but twice. When Kedorlaomer rallies three other kings to join him against Sodom and Gomorrah, they take Lot prisoner. God indirectly rescues Lot through Abraham's intervention with his army.[8] This salvation event should have awakened Lot to the fact that he'd chosen his new home poorly; blessing and security were found with his faithful relative. But Lot learned nothing; after his rescue, he returned to Sodom.[9] Have you ever ignored a clear warning from God, only to wish later that you'd paid more attention?

Despite Lot's recklessness in ignoring the consequences of his choices, God did not leave him to his own devices. Instead, God directly intervened to rescue Lot right before he destroyed Sodom and Gomorrah. God sent two angels who knew that destroying the cities was their only option. But before they did, they were determined to liberate Lot.[10] First, the angels warned him of what they were about to do and urged him to leave the city. After ignoring the first warning when Abraham rescued him, this second angelic warning is pure mercy. This shows you something of God's attitude toward Lot: he longs for Lot to listen.

And yet, the next sentence begins, "With the coming of dawn."[11] Somehow Lot has dallied the night away and still is not ready to go. He

---

8 Gen. 14:13-16.
9 Gen. 19:1.
10 Gen. 19:1-29.
11 Gen. 19:15.

has taken mercy for granted a second time. At that point the angels urge him to "Hurry!" – a third warning to get moving.

If I had been in Lot's place, I don't know that I would really need any more urging. The night before, the townspeople were prepared to break down his door before the angels intervened and blinded the crowd. Would you need more reason to leave? Apparently Lot does. And (this should amaze you – let it sink in!) he gets the additional warning. God stoops, unnecessarily, to provide Lot with help that matches his need. And he doesn't grumble, lose his temper, or complain. You cannot fake that kind of goodness. Look at the heart God is showing you!

Even then, however, the next verse begins, "When he [Lot] hesitated . . . ."[12] What is he waiting for? Back in college, as my friends and I were trying to discern God's will for our lives, we would talk about how nice it would be if he would send us a sign we could not miss or misinterpret. We joked that a couple of angels would be helpful. Better yet, angels carrying a flashing neon sign that said, "Go this way!" with an arrow. We never got the sign, but Lot sure did. Yet he still hesitates.

How could Lot be so clueless? Unfortunately, it's pretty easy. When you first get a warning, you take it seriously. Like Lot, you might even act on it initially. But if you need a warning, it means you're already partially blind, so it doesn't take much to completely close your eyes. You begin to think, *It's not too late.* Then *I still have time* becomes *I'll get around to it.* And then the warning is forgotten.

In that sense, Lot is Everyman; he doesn't know how to act in his own best interests. But cluelessness does not relieve us of responsibility. Lot has ignored God's warnings. Now if I were God, I would have had enough: "Okay, Lot. You really don't want to leave? Fine! You die too. You have worked hard enough to identify with these people in life, so you might as well go all the way!" You might share my uncharitable attitude, but the passage requires us to realize that God does not.

The angels grab Lot, his wife, and his daughters and force them to leave the city. Why? "For the LORD was merciful to them."[13] Do you see God's heart here? He may be exasperated by Lot – we're not told – but he's not ready to quit the way I would be. With Lot, God's mercy takes on a whole new depth of meaning because God chose to paint it on a canvas that you and I would have scrapped a long time ago. Familiar phrases like "God, who is rich in mercy"[14] have more punch than they did before. Maybe I can believe that God is not ready to quit on me either.

---

[12] Gen. 19:16.
[13] Gen. 19:16.
[14] Eph. 2:4.

Read on and God will show you even more of his heart. "As soon as they had brought them out, one of them said, 'Flee for your lives! Don't look back, and don't stop anywhere in the plain! Flee to the mountains or you will be swept away!'"[15] That seems clear (and emphatic) enough! Then the next verse begins, "But Lot said . . . ." Here is a guy who just doesn't get it. "But Lot said to them, 'No, my lords, please! Your servant has found favor in your eyes, and you have shown great kindness to me in sparing my life. But I can't flee to the mountains; this disaster will overtake me, and I'll die. Look, here is a town near enough to run to, and it is small. Let me flee to it – it is very small, isn't it? Then my life will be spared.'"[16]

Even as Lot reluctantly leaves and is exhorted to flee for his life, he still drags his feet. Instead of running as fast as he can, he tries to bargain with the angels. The Lord of the universe has decided to wipe out a loathsome spot on a wayward planet and Lot still thinks he can negotiate!

Once again it should amaze you that the Lord listens. He responds by saying, "Very well, I will grant this request too."[17] This is not a story about a doomed social climber; it is a rich story of a wonderful God. Not only does he put up with stubborn people, he bends low and cares about their needs. His faithfulness is shot through with compassion, kindness, and patience.

What do you see in this passage? You see sorry and pathetic people, the kind Jerry Springer invites you to laugh at and hold in contempt. But you also see a wonderful God, who does not mock, laugh, or use their failings to inflate his own sense of importance. You see a God of all grace.

God tells you stories about wretched people who can neither see nor do what is best for themselves or their families. In the telling, God tells you even more about himself. People make life hard on God. They doubt him, ignore him, disobey him, and are miserable to him. And in his response, you see God extend his sovereignty, power, and might on their behalf. He is kind to the undeserving.

Do you know yourself as undeserving? If so, take heart. Here is a God who not only remains committed to his people despite their failings, but does so with compassion.

That's a God who melts my heart. I am also a stubborn, foolish, reckless man who does not always do what is best for me and for my family. I am lured by the world and resist God's warnings. What gives me hope is knowing that I have a God whose compassion is greater than my foolishness.

---

15 Gen. 19:17.
16 Gen. 19:18-20.
17 Gen. 19:21.

Modern Day Lot

Martin was experiencing that compassion. He had received – and ignored – God's warnings for years and was now reaping the consequences. Ruined relationships littered his path like leaves, yet God had not abandoned him. He sensed God's nearness when he was lonely, God's strength when he was tempted, and God's courage when he had to do and say difficult things to deal with problems he had caused. As much as he deserved otherwise, he knew that God had not abandoned him. He was grateful and encouraged by the evidence that God still loved him.

But it was a bittersweet encouragement given the devastation he was experiencing. With a pained look and just a trace of resentment, he asked one day, "Why didn't God get my attention earlier and do this in an easier way?"

The answer was obvious – God had – but it would be hard for Martin to admit. No one plans to take God's warnings for granted. It happens subtly. We all experience the warnings but talk about how "lucky" we are to dodge a bullet. When we speak like that, God's mercy becomes impersonal, disconnected from him and from his heart. We may give theological assent to the fact that he is sovereign, but we often talk as if the world runs itself. We close our eyes to what he tries to show us. Martin hadn't planned to disregard God's warnings, but he had just the same.

With all the compassion I felt for him as he sat examining his life's debris, I said, "God did try to get your attention. But you ignored him." Martin slowly nodded in agreement. My comment would have been cruel had it come from an enemy, but Martin knew I was his friend. And because he'd been seeing that God was too, he could hear the truth about himself without being ripped apart. When you know that God is not fed up with you even when others are, it helps you accept the wrecked parts of your life without being destroyed by them. You can get up and go on with hope for the present and the future.

How can you avoid the path of Lot or Martin? How do you step off the elevator before it reaches the basement? You begin by taking God's heart seriously. He warns you because he cares for you. Mercy originates with a person; therefore, you must recognize mercy as personal. You haven't been "lucky"; you've been spoken to by the living God who has your best interests in mind. Respond to him. Thank him for his kindness in warning you. Acknowledge that he's the One who rescued you. Thank him for having a heart for you. Such faith responses will guard you from taking him for granted.

on your own

1   In what unique way(s) do your typical sin patterns complicate relationships? How does your special "talent" (i.e. stubborn streaks, laziness, chronic indifference, critical nature, glory hog, man-pleaser, self-righteousness, truth hiding) make it hard for others and for God to relate to you?

2   How has God been kind to you anyway? How has his graciousness matched your need? Where has he rescued you from yourself? Take some time to reflect on his mercy to you. Allow his kindness to break your heart.

3   How would your relationships with Jesus and others change if that difficult part of you began to change?

4   Go back and read other Bible stories that we typically think revolve around people (such as Jacob, Noah, any of the judges or kings, and Jonah), this time with an eye toward the way God reveals himself. What does he reveal? This will be too good to keep to yourself, so think carefully, and then share your discoveries with a friend.

Part II

God calms
your fears

At times we distrust God's kindness toward his people; at other times we actively believe he is against us. Part I focused on passive unbelief – our failure to see God's good heart. In this section, we will look at the active unbelief that attributes evil motives to God as he deals with his people; the belief that he intends to hurt us or refuses to receive us.

We often get into trouble by pitting certain attributes and activities of God (i.e. holiness, judgment, and wrath) against those that are more immediately appealing (i.e. mercy, reconciliation, and faithfulness). Chapters 6 and 7 address our fears about God's anger by showing how it does not contradict his more gracious attributes when he deals with his people. Another way we can distort our relationship with God is by doubting he will receive us unless our faith is perfectly unwavering. Chapters 8 through 10 may surprise you as you see the way God responds to people who have feeble faith or even active doubt.

Are you scared he'll hurt you when he's angry?

Anger keeps people off balance. You never know what an angry person is going to say or do, but there's a pretty high probability that it will be unpleasant and hurtful in some way.

For several years I worked in an inner city ministry with people who could not get or keep jobs because of their struggles with various addictions. For them, anger was a way of life.

Take Tonya as an example. Her personality was larger than life. She awed me, coming as I did from a small town, simply by walking into the room. Tonya calm had a presence you could not overlook. But Tonya upset was frightening – loud, unrestrained, and abusive. When Tonya wasn't happy, she let you know it, especially if she was unhappy with *you*. She did not weigh her words before speaking, and she lived with more inner turmoil than peace. Everyone breathed a bit easier when she missed a day at work.

Colin, however, was worse. A young man whose primary education came from the streets, Colin learned early the power of intimidating rage. My ministry partner invited him to live with us and suddenly life got a lot harder. One morning we woke up to discover that our microwave, bicycles, and other things had disappeared – along with Colin. He had sold them to finance a drug binge. When we told him he had to move out for awhile, he blew up, punched a hole in an office door, and stormed out, vowing that we'd pay. His tactic worked. I lived fearfully for a long time, wondering what he might do. The last I heard, he was in prison for murder.

Angry people purposely create an unsafe environment. They promise to hurt you if you don't do as they wish. Forget about moving closer or sharing your life with them. Though they are unpredictable in many ways, you can be sure that, eventually, they will use whatever you share against you. My honest (though not terribly godly) first response to such people is, "The less involvement I have, the better." I don't like or trust angry people.

Working *with* angry people is miserable, but it's worse when you work *for* them. An angry boss has the power to hurt you in ways ordinary people don't, and you can't just walk away. It's a very uncomfortable situation that makes relationship impossible as you insulate yourself from attack. The more interaction you have, the more nastiness you receive.

God's angry side frightens many people. They read the Bible and realize that among angry people, God is the angriest. That anger puts an edge on all his other attributes – his authority, power, and complete control over all creation. Sure, he's majestic and glorious – and dangerous. Each time I speak about how well God treats sinners, someone asks how his anger fits into the picture. Perhaps his anger makes it hard for you to open up and trust him. If you cannot trust him, his power and might remain downright frightening.

EVERYONE IN THE HANDS OF AN ANGRY GOD

God is angry fairly often and the scale of his judgment is devastating. In the Old Testament, for instance, God responds to pervasive human wickedness with a global flood, horrific plagues against Egypt, and the destruction of the Canaanites. You quickly learn that you don't mess around with God. Holiness and obedience are not optional. He means what he says and metes out consequences for disobedience. And it's not only pagans who bear his wrath. God also gets angry with the Israelites when they idolize the golden calf, doubt him in the desert, and stray from him repeatedly throughout the reigns of many kings.

Anger, wrath, and judgment are part of who God is. As we read such accounts, however, we would be wrong to assume that *similar* emotional responses are actually *identical*. That is, we would be wrong to assume that anger is anger — that all anger is the same. That assumption is terrifying! Because if God is angry with all people in the same way, what will keep him from wiping *us* out? This fear erodes our faith and keeps us from being vulnerable with God. How could you dare come near an angry God to deal with the ways you've made him angry?

But you can. You do so by realizing that God is not angry with his people in the same way he is with those who are not. If we equate flood and Egypt anger with golden calf and wilderness anger, we will lose confidence that God will remain faithful to us. So we need to understand how these angers differ.

FAITHLESS, NOT REBELLIOUS

One helpful place to begin is an often overlooked passage where Zelophehad's daughters come to Moses, arguing that their family should receive an inheritance even though they had no male heir.[1] For the Israelites, land was vitally important. It was part of their promised inheritance as the people of God, a visible down payment that showed they were part of God's kingdom. Without land, a person's name disappeared from among God's people and no longer shared in Abraham's inheritance. He did not belong to the people who belong to God! Zelophehad's daughters are raising a serious concern about their place in God's covenant.

They say to Moses, "Our father died in the desert. He was not among Korah's followers, who banded together against the LORD, but he died for his own sin and left no sons."[2] In other words, they argue that he was faithless, not rebellious. What do you think – is that a legitimate distinction or just word games? How willingly would you accept your seven-year-old's argument that "I didn't really lie, I only stretched the truth"? Oddly enough, however, God sides with the daughters. He indicates that they have correctly understood the core issue. True, their father had weak faith – he didn't believe God could bring him into the Promised Land – but he did not try to supplant God's authority with an alternate leader. Therefore, God agrees that Zelophehad's name should continue so he grants his daughters land. Zelophehad – and his family – belonged!

Zelophehad experienced God's anger but not the kind that destroyed his name or his family. Though disciplined for his faithlessness by wandering in the desert for forty years, he remained part of the covenant community. In the end, his family inherited along with everyone else. The divine anger he experienced did not eternally annihilate him. Instead, God intended that suffering to train Zelophehad to trust him better.[3] In short, Zelophehad experienced gracious anger.

FAITHLESS AND REBELLIOUS

God's anger is different when he deals with those outside his covenant community. But because we don't always see this distinction, we wind up misinterpreting certain passages and distorting the true character of our Lord as a result.

---

[1] Num. 27:1-7.
[2] Num. 27:3.
[3] Deut. 8:2-5.

For example, you may be familiar with the story of Achan out of the book of Joshua.[4] After the battle of Jericho, Achan takes clothes and gold from the city and hides them in his tent, though it was all supposed to be either destroyed or placed in the sanctuary treasury. The army then lost its next battle because Achan stole from and disobeyed the Lord.

It's a straightforward story, but the application can be tricky. We scratch our heads, thinking, *Well, what got Achan into trouble was secretly hiding things he wanted but should not have had. So I need to be careful not to hide things either. If I sin, I need to come out into the light with it before God destroys me or my family.* Your experience likely supports such logic. Remember those times you decided to live a secretly disobedient life – lying about whom you dated or where you went, how much money you actually spent on that dress, or your internet pornography addiction? Remember too how those secrets threatened or ruined your life? You may even be hiding things right now that will destroy you, secrets you know you need to confess.

The problem with using the Achan passage to prod you into confessing sin is that you don't end up with a great deal of confidence in God's mercy. It feels more like a sword hanging over your head: "Better 'fess up fast before God breaks down your door!" Remember that the erosion of our confidence in God's kindness comes from misinterpreting God's anger for someone who is part of his family as opposed to someone who isn't. In this case, I'm not at all sure that Achan is part of the covenant community.

You may be thinking, *Wait a minute! How can you say he's not part of the covenant community? His family came out of Egypt and wandered with Israel in the desert. Achan himself served in the army. Of course he's part of the covenant community!*

Look, though, at what happened to him. Achan, along with his family and possessions, was taken outside the camp to be stoned and burned. As you turn away from that awful scene, you're left with a mental picture of a pile of smoking rocks. What a striking parallel to Jericho's destruction one chapter earlier! After its walls collapsed, it too was set on fire, leaving only a heap of smoking rubble.[5] Achan shares the fate of the non-covenant community. Because his fate and theirs are the same, the author of Joshua is directing you to see that Achan has more in common with Jericho than he does with the covenant community.

---

[4] Josh. 7:1-26.
[5] I am indebted to John Timlin for drawing my attention to these parallels.

Therefore, this is not intended to be a passage about God's people dealing with personal hidden sins. It is about how some people live in the middle of the covenant community yet aren't really members of it. They may say the right things and hang out with the right people, but their hearts are not inclined to honor the Lord as holy. When push comes to shove, they are just along for the ride. When temptation comes, they will satisfy their own desires instead of obeying the Lord. This passage strongly warns, "Look at what you do with God's commands. That will indicate to which community you really belong!"

This warning is underscored when you compare Achan's story with the story of Rahab a few chapters earlier.[6] There you are told about someone who lives among the heathen in Jericho but actually belongs to the people of God. She demonstrates her faith by hiding the spies Joshua sends, risking her own life to serve the Lord. Achan demonstrates his faithlessness by hiding plunder he stole to serve himself.

God's anger at Achan is not what believers should expect. Achan's story is a warning to complacent people who don't exhibit evidence of faith; it's not an encouragement to the faithful to repent.[7] We get into trouble when we believe that the way God deals with Achan is the way he deals with believers.

My purpose in discussing Achan's story has been to highlight the different types of God's anger, not to increase your anxiety about whether or not you are part of God's family. If you find yourself distracted by such questions, take a moment to consider Revelation 16. As God pours out the very last vestiges of his righteous wrath on a rebellious planet, we're told that the people experiencing it curse him repeatedly and refuse to repent. There lies the key as you consider your own interaction with God's just anger: when you experience it, does it lead you to repent or to harden yourself against him? If you more clearly see your faults, more strongly hate them, and long to turn from them, then Achan's story need not cause you to fear.

A PLACE FOR GRACE

What a contrast between Achan and Zelophehad! Achan's family is destroyed along with him and, therefore, he doesn't receive any land in Canaan. His name is no longer registered among the chosen people. Achan bears the full weight of his own sin – as do those caught in the flood, in Egypt, and in Canaan – and is destroyed.

---

[6] Josh. 2:1-24; 6:22-25.
[7] Rev. 16:9, 11, 21.

For the people of God, we see an entirely different outcome. Each time God is angry with his people, something happens so that they do not bear its full weight. Sacrifices are offered as atonement. Moses prays, intercedes, and asks that the people be spared. Aaron offers incense before God and stands between God's people and God's plague. Those two aspects of grace – intercession and atonement – appear throughout Scripture to absorb the explosive impact of human sin meeting a righteous and just God.

Ultimately Christ comes, satisfying God's wrath in a way that all the sacrifices and weak human intercessors could not. Jesus drains the cup of God's wrath against his people once for all so that there isn't even a drop left for his people.[8] God will not stay angry forever. For those who hate and curse him, he pours out anger as punishment. When it is concluded, he declares, "It is done"[9] though it takes an eternity for them to absorb it. Jesus also uttered, "It is finished" when he exhausted God's wrath on behalf of his people.[10] One way or another, the Father's anger finishes. Either people exhaust it themselves or a substitute does.

Notice God's kindness in dealing with sinners. In love, he finds a way to deal with the anger his people provoke, even though it means that he must bear the punishment his righteous wrath requires. He pays so that Zelophehad did not. He pays so that you do not. The consequences you suffer are not intended to pay God back. In that sense, they are not punishment, but rather training so that you might learn to live a holy life.

My son struggles to understand the difference between punishment and training. The other day he began batting balls around the living room in frustration because they were not cooperating in a project he was building. My response was to take away the toys, since it was not the first time we had talked about this kind of behavior, and I was angry at having to do it again. Several minutes later, my son came and placed his most special, favorite stuffed animal in my lap and sobbed, "I think you should take Doggy too."

My heart broke. Somehow, my expressions of ungodly anger, combined with his innate penitential bent, led him to believe that he has to pay something to make my anger go away. He doesn't understand that I have no desire for him to pay anything back. He doesn't understand that, in my best moments, I discipline him for what I believe is his best, not because I expect him to pay a debt he has incurred.

---

8 This favorite picture of C. John Miller's loses nothing for its multiple retellings.

9 Rev. 16:17.

10 John 19:30.

Do you struggle like this with God? Are you unsure how to deal with his anger? Perhaps you find yourself holding back when you sin, avoiding devotional times or God's people because you're not sure what God might do. Or maybe you're afraid: you know such thoughts are silly, but you're afraid that if you confess what you've done, he'll punish you for it. Have you ever expected him to take away something you loved because of some wrong you had done? All of those faith struggles mirror my son's conviction that I want to ruin his life when I'm angry. God does get angry, but even his anger leads to good ends for his people.

Anger that disciplines is different from anger that destroys. Such anger speaks of a holy God's grace to people who don't deserve it. It's corrective, not destructive. More than that, being angry with family costs God, and he willingly pays the price. You don't need to be afraid of this awesome, powerful God, because he pays what you never could. That's a God you can have great confidence in, even when you've angered him.

on your own

1   When you are reluctant to turn to God, what are you scared of? Actively fight your fear by confessing to Jesus that you don't fully believe he will receive you.

2   The crucifixion of Christ is the place where God's anger against his people was poured out. Meditate on what it means that Jesus took all your punishment and that there is no more – even though you keep sinning. How does that change the way you approach God? Be careful not to view Christ's sacrifice as a get-out-of-jail-free card. To do so would be to gravely misunderstand what it cost Christ, and most likely represents a shallow relationship with him. If, however, you are profoundly moved to gratefulness, then rest assured, there is no more wrath for you.

3   Write down the differences between punishment and discipline. (Hebrews 12:4-12 may be helpful.) Understanding this distinction is important for your relationship with God. What are God's goals in training his people? How does discipline factor into those goals? What do you not need to fear when God disciplines you? What do you need to remember?

4   Ask a few friends to share times in their lives when they were scared of God and how that has changed for them. Ask them to tell you stories of how they were surprised by his kindness or surprised to receive forgiveness when they expected punishment. Ask them to tell you what has helped them grow in confidence over the years: passages they have studied, theology that has come alive, meaningful songs they have sung, books they have read, etc.

Are you afraid he'll threaten you to make you behave?

'I've been saying that you don't need to be afraid of God, but sometimes the Bible does seem to suggest that he's willing to scare his people into obedience. A good example is the giving of the Ten Commandments.[1] The Israelites had just escaped from Egypt, passed through the Red Sea, and traveled to Mount Sinai. There God promised to speak with them, but not until they properly prepared. God gave them three days to consecrate and purify themselves. They were instructed to wash their clothes but also to take time to develop the right mindset.

It's hard not to wonder what was in their minds as they got ready because there was an ominous side to their preparations. The Israelites had to cordon off the mountain so that no creature could go near it. They were told to stone to death any animal or human that touched the mountain. You can almost hear them thinking, *What kind of God is this? He destroys Egypt and now we will die if we go near him.*

Finally, as the great day dawned, thunder, lightening, and a thick cloud wreathed the mountain. Then came a very loud trumpet blast, causing the people to tremble. Summoned by the trumpet, they went to the foot of the mountain now covered with smoke like that from a furnace. The mountain trembled violently as the trumpet got louder and louder. Do you have the picture? Clearly, meeting with God went well beyond what the Israelites could control, and perhaps beyond what they could endure. At that moment of maximum, terrifying anticipation, God spoke and the people unraveled. They trembled with fear, stayed at a distance, and said to Moses, "Speak to us yourself and we will listen. But do not have God speak to us or we will die."[2]

---

[1] Ex. 19:2-21.
[2] Ex. 20:18-19.

Do What's Right, or Else!

Fear is a powerful motivator of good behavior. I was talking with a wonderful, godly woman once about the difficulties of raising children. This sweet, cheerful grandmother looked puzzled as we talked, and then her face suddenly hardened. With a stern look she said, "You know, Bill, we didn't have problems like many parents today because my kids feared my husband."

She is not alone in believing that we need to scare our kids into obeying. Have you ever towered over your child to demonstrate how much bigger you are? You wouldn't do this unless you believed that the implied threat of your size helped emphasize your point. The same is true when you shout at your kids, communicating with volume that you are more than they want to challenge. When those techniques fail, you might threaten the loss of a privilege to keep them obedient: "Do that again, and no dessert!" Others threaten physical violence: "Just wait until your father gets home . . . ." Still others simply lash out physically without warning, creating an ongoing threat of physical pain. I wish I could say even one of these scare tactics was alien to my experience of parenting. What makes such techniques appealing? When you're at the end of your rope, sometimes making your kids fear you seems like the only way to keep your sanity.

The problem, however, with fear as a governing technique is that it motivates people to avoid consequences, not to love and honor those in charge. Consider what happens in a police state. Nearly everybody toes the line while only a few violate the rules. But people obey only because the punishments are severe, not because they believe their government cares for them. They are coerced into obeying and as history repeatedly shows, those governed that way only wait for, look for, or create an opportunity to change their governors. The same instability plagues families that rely on intimidation to maintain order.

Many people believe, however, that fearing the consequences of disobedience is what God wants us to do. Instead of developing greater confidence that he will handle their failings well, they grow in fear as their sins increase. When they obey, they do so slavishly, not gratefully or joyfully. Such a pattern is non-relational at its foundation and not what God wants. But isn't God trying to coerce obedience at Mt. Sinai?

Notice that not all the Israelites responded to God in the same way. Moses' response was different from the rest. Moses too, was overwhelmed by what he experienced. As Hebrews 12:21 records, he too trembled with fear. And yet, in that awesome, fearful moment, Moses said something that, given the context, is unbelievable. As this terrifying experience reached its crescendo and the Israelites sensed their imminent destruction, Moses spoke to the people and said, "Do not be afraid."[3]

Do not be afraid?! Considering the unbridled power that God has just unleashed, fear seems to be one of the few appropriate responses. Can you hear the Israelites thinking, *Do not be afraid? Are you nuts? Don't you see and hear the same things we do? How can anyone not be afraid?*

Moses finished his sentence, "Do not be afraid. God has come to test you, so that the fear of God will be with you to keep you from sinning." Did I hear him correctly? Did he just say, "Don't be afraid, yet your fear will protect you from sinning?" Hmmm . . . maybe Moses is so scared he's no longer coherent. How are you supposed to fear, yet not be afraid? Which instruction are you supposed to follow?

The wordsmiths among us might wonder if there is a play on words in the passage, in which the Hebrew word for "afraid" is different from the word for "fear." But the Hebrew root is the same for both words. Yet clearly, Moses is distinguishing between two kinds of fear. He recognizes that the Israelites are displaying a bad kind of fear that needs to be replaced with a good kind. Examining the context more closely will help us to better understand what's happening.

Think again about the Israelites' response to God's proclamation: "Do not have God speak to us or we will die."[4] They feared being destroyed by God. They were convinced he would use his power and glory against them in the same way he had crushed their enemies. Moses responded essentially by saying, "Do not be afraid – you will not die." In other words, "You've misunderstood God's purpose." God did not want his children to be scared that he would destroy them. He did not reveal himself in order to terrify them into obedience.

It's important to understand that terror is all about control. It is not about helping others to become better people or be better prepared to handle the challenges of life. You don't benefit when someone scares you to death; it doesn't help you care for others or be more considerate. Instead, you learn to avoid scary people, or at least avoid the scary consequences of upsetting them. If you are frightened that someone might hurt you, you are less likely to think, say, or do anything that would upset him. You end up wrapping your life around someone else

---

3 Ex. 20:20.
4 Ex. 20:19.

to avoid a negative reaction. Fear, terror, and fright are light-years from true heartfelt obedience. No one will ever scare you into goodness.

There is little that grieves me more than when my children obey only because they're frightened of the consequences. They need consequences at times, but I'd prefer my children to obey me because they trust that I have good reasons for what I'm saying, even if they don't understand them. If fear is what restrains their foolishness, then that foolishness lies dormant within them and never gets replaced by wisdom. At some point, this sleeping foolishness will wake up. My children will mature – mentally, emotionally, and physically – beyond the reach of any consequence I'm able to impose. If they haven't learned to love godliness, then they will pursue folly to their own injury.

Fear never motivates true godliness. If it could, God would have little problem producing holiness in his people. Humans typically fall apart when they catch a glimpse of God unmasked. Isaiah came unglued when he saw God in the temple.[5] The disciples were terrified when Jesus was transfigured.[6] John fainted when he saw the risen Christ in all his glory on Patmos.[7] Instilling terror would be easy for God, but that's not the way he wants to relate to his people. Even in the immensely frightening scene at Mount Sinai, God longed for something other than the slavish fear his people offered him. That fear would only get in the way of loving and serving him. It had more in common with mindless terror than it did with what Peter describes as "reverent fear."[8]

Reverent Fear

Reverent fear recognizes who God is and respects his authority. After all, Jesus says that God can throw you into hell.[9] You don't need to fear that he will do this, but you need to respect his power to do so. Instead of driving you away, reverent fear can actually draw you nearer to God. Your confidence that he will not destroy you, even though you deserve it, produces thankfulness to him because mercy waits for you instead of destruction. You love God more and don't take his mercy for granted. Reverent fear allows you to hate sin while having confidence that Christ will receive you when you fall.

At Mount Sinai, the Israelites saw God's power and glory, but forgot the underlying grace and kindness that seasons the way he uses his

---

5 Isa. 6:5.
6 Matt. 17:6.
7 Rev. 1:17.
8 1 Peter 1:17.
9 Mark 9:47.

awesome power. What they needed – and what they had – was a mediator who could speak for God to them. They needed someone who would stand between them and God, someone who would help them understand God and know how to respond to him. They needed to know that God did not desire for them to live in abject terror, that he was approachable. At the same moment, they needed to be exhorted not to take him lightly but to obey him with reverent fear.

God chose a mediator who would meet their exact need at that precise moment. You too have a Mediator who is also your God. As he saw the desperate need of Jerusalem, Jesus longed to gather his people under his protection.[10] His people rejected him, but do you see his great love for them? His heart and his longing have not changed. He does not rule with terror. Rather, he invites you to come to him with reverent confidence when you need his mercy and his help[11] – because he is just like his Father.

---

[10] Matt. 23:37-39.
[11] Heb. 4:16.

on your own

1   How has misunderstanding God's anger affected you? How has it affected
    your view of him and your relationship with him?

2   Remember a time when you were motivated to obey God out of unholy
    fear. Think about the effects this had. How effective was terror in helping
    you develop lifelong obedience that was pleasing to God? What parts of
    the gospel did your fear cause you to ignore? Did being scared enable you
    to grow in confidence in Christ and his work in you?

3   Think about people you have tried to coerce into doing what was right.
    Have you ever inappropriately threatened that God would harm someone
    if he or she didn't get in line with your agenda? These are hard things to
    recognize because threats often produce what we want to see, but only in
    the short term. In the long term, such threats usually backfire, undoing rela-
    tionships. Confess these times to God, asking for his forgiveness for deal-
    ing with people so differently than the way he has with you.

4   You may also need to go to someone you've wronged and ask for his or
    her forgiveness. Talk this over with a wise friend first to gain wisdom on
    how and when to go to another appropriately.

Do you suspect he'll only help you if you help yourself?

Ungodly fear can keep us from approaching God for help, but so too can a deep shame about our own unworthiness. At times, you might have said to yourself, *You've ignored God for years, doing whatever you wanted. You don't deserve his help now!* Our hearts tend to believe that we should only get what we deserve. Since we deserve hell, why would we even think of asking for help? We certainly wouldn't extend mercy to someone who had treated us as poorly as we have treated God.

AN UNWORTHY PLAINTIFF

As an extreme example, consider a prostitute who has been robbed and tries to recover her property through legal channels. Think about how uncomfortable she might feel as she entered the courtroom. What hope would she have that she would be believed, respected, and helped? You might give her credit for having the nerve to try, but success would be a miracle. What a miserable position to be in: an outcast needing help but unable to demand it and unlikely to get it. Yet that is the backdrop for the case that established King Solomon's legendary stature as the wisest man on earth.

Surprised? Did you ever notice that the court case he presided over in 1 Kings 3 involved two prostitutes squabbling over an illegitimate son? These details escaped my notice for decades. For some reason when I was growing up, we never focused on either woman's identity in Sunday school! Their profession escaped my notice and may have escaped yours, but it didn't escape God's. In fact, God looked down and said, "That's the perfect setting to display my wisdom and justice! Tell this story so that my people can learn about me and their faith won't be impoverished!" And so the greatness and breadth of Solomon's wisdom has forever been established by a dispute he mediated between two prostitutes.

It's important to understand why Solomon requested wisdom from God and why this request is, in itself, astounding. Have you ever longed to be Aladdin and receive three wishes from the magic lamp? Solomon is the only person who actually had such an opportunity.[1] He could have had anything he wanted from God – wealth, long life, freedom from his enemies – and he chose . . . wisdom.

Let's be honest: doesn't his choice feel like a let-down? It's like receiving a beautifully wrapped Christmas present. You undo the ribbon, tear off the paper, find a knife to cut the tape around the opening – your anticipation building with each moment – and pull off the top to discover an olive-colored ceramic pickle dish that matches nothing you own. In fact, you can't imagine any décor where this dish would feel at home. You say to the giver, "Oh! . . . Thank you. It's, um, lovely!" Then you rack your brain for a place to stash it until you can safely recycle it at the thrift store. Solomon's request for wisdom feels a bit like that. What he got was nice, but couldn't he have requested something better, something more practical or exciting?

For Solomon's choice to make more sense, we need to better understand wisdom's essence: a deep, penetrating understanding of the world and how it works. Wisdom lets you see the world from God's point of view and act in harmony with the way he made things. Instead of fighting against God in his universe, you work along with him. Wisdom encompasses everything, including the ability to perceive the truth regarding people. You understand what moves them, fools them, trips them up. You can interact with them in ways that are beneficial, not destructive. Solomon seeks wisdom because he knows that leading Israel goes well beyond his ability. Without help, he will be unable to lead in a way that lines up with God's plans or helps God's people. God thinks well of Solomon's request and grants it. Solomon's wisdom will bless God's people and will benefit Solomon as well. Instead of an odd-looking pickle dish, Solomon has unwrapped a beautiful crystal chandelier that will provide light, beautify his home, and delight his guests.

And the first time we see this beautiful, practical gift, it is being used to help . . . prostitutes. Wasn't there a better defining moment available to showcase his wisdom? Why not highlight the great temples and

---

[1] 1 Kings 3:5.

palaces Solomon built to demonstrate the glory of God's kingdom? Or the heads of state who came from afar to consult with the wisest of men? Or the magnificent worship service Solomon organized? Solomon used his wisdom for all these things, but not until after it had been established through a seedy story fit for a daytime talk show. We know that God has not lost his aversion to prostitution. The Torah is clear about its evils, and later prophetic literature describes Israel's flagrant unfaithfulness to God in these same terms.[2] Yet despite the immoral context, God includes this story in Scripture because its absence would weaken your faith. It's probably time for us to take another look.

WOMAN OF THE NIGHT

The prostitute who brought her case to Solomon would not have anything to commend her to the judge. She may have turned to prostitution because of desperate circumstances, but prostitution was not her only option. In contrast, Naomi's daughter-in-law, Ruth, chose gleaning over a disreputable life, even as a destitute alien. So the woman in Solomon's court was not simply a victim of circumstances. As a professional, she intentionally and repeatedly offered herself for profit.

This being so, hasn't this woman simply reaped what she has sown? She keeps evil company in an immoral occupation. Little wonder that another prostitute would steal her child and lie about it. On one level, couldn't this be God's judgment against her, or the natural consequence of sinful choices? Wouldn't it serve her right to watch her child being raised by a woman who accidentally smothered her own baby? How well do you think this other woman will provide for a child she knows isn't hers when she couldn't take care of her own? The agony seems to fit the larger crime: she has shown little concern for those made in God's image (herself and her customers); now she'll have to watch someone show little concern for a child made in hers. Rough justice to be sure, but just nonetheless, right?

It's also not surprising that she has no one to speak on her behalf or force the other woman to return her child. Why should someone else get involved and get caught up in guilt by association? Speak up for her and you too could be viewed as disreputable and unworthy of compassion. This woman's problems are all due to her lifestyle. She is getting what's coming to her. It may make sense to our way of thinking . . . but not to God's.

---

2 For example, see Lev. 19:29, Deut. 31:16, and Jer. 3:1-13.

God sees her as someone who needs help – who is weak, impotent, and powerless – and unlikely to get it. She has no right to expect justice, yet God through Solomon exposes the other woman as an imposter and returns the baby to his true mother. He cares about her and her child. He doesn't allow her enemy to get away with negligence and kidnapping. He sets the world right again.

Part of the world being correctly realigned means that a disreputable woman gets kindness. God isn't simply kind to the so-called deserving poor. He doesn't only help those who help themselves. Here the riches of his wisdom are lavished on a person many of us would not invite into our homes. It is a foretaste of what Paul describes in Ephesians 2, where God makes alive those who were dead in their sin, people who lived according to the passions of the sinful nature and carried out the desires of their bodies and minds. People who had nothing to commend themselves to God and who were fully responsible for their condition. People like me and you.

Do you see yourself in the prostitute's shoes? Do you realize that, when God uses prostitutes to illustrate Israel's unfaithfulness to him, he's showing you yourself?[3] He's talking about you. One of your primary identities is "unfaithful." Sexual immorality as a metaphor is not confined to the Old Testament. James also uses the image to illustrate the heart of our spiritual problems when he calls believers spiritual adulterers.[4] Like paid professionals, we too are repeatedly and intentionally faithless, bearing the consequences in destroyed relationships, both human and divine.

Do you see yourself creating many of your deepest problems while at the same time eliminating any hope for their resolution? Do you realize that, before God, you don't deserve help? It's miserable to realize that the train wrecks of your life are mostly of your own making. It's a hopeless place to be, where taking your lumps, giving up, or ignoring your problems seem like the only alternatives. And yet, the woman in Solomon's court did something different. She hoped. She believed. She had faith. And that faith changed her life.

She had the courage to believe that she could be heard and helped despite who she was and what she had done. She had the heart to believe that she would be received, and she was right. Her hope was not disappointed. Hope was the only thing she had going for her and, mercifully, hope was enough.

---

[3] Ezek. 16.
[4] James 4:4.

Today we know that Solomon's wisdom was supreme because he used it on behalf of a social outcast. This story is about wisdom, but specifically as it is used to grant mercy and justice to the undeserving. If you can see that you are not so different – that you too are undeserving and in desperate need of God's help – then you also can confidently hope that God will receive you and help you.

NOT ALL IN THE DARK WANT LIGHT

Unlike this prostitute, however, some people expect nothing from God. They don't believe he will receive them and they don't believe they will find mercy. They expect judgment or, at best, a harsh response from God that says, "You've made your bed, now lie in it!" Because of their false expectations, they don't come. They refuse to believe God is telling the truth when he invites them, so they do not find mercy in their times of trouble. They do not believe God.

Others assume that they don't really need very much from God. They cannot identify with the woman at court. In fact, the story rubs them the wrong way: "This isn't right! Good people should be rewarded and bad people should pay for what they've done. Won't Solomon's verdict simply convince the woman that her lifestyle pays off? Solomon should have lectured both women on the wages of sin and sent them packing!"

If you find it too difficult to identify with this woman, beware! When Jesus tells the parable of the prodigal son,[5] he only lets you identify with one of two people – the reckless prodigal who knows what he is and what he needs, or the self-righteous older brother whose hard heart has no room for mercy. But we all need mercy! Those who don't realize this are in danger of mimicking the Pharisee's prayer, "God, I thank you that I am not like other men – robbers, evildoers, adulterers – or even like this tax collector."[6] Elsewhere, Jesus tells a Pharisee, who complained when Jesus allowed a woman of the street to touch him, that he (the Pharisee) was the one whose sins were not forgiven.[7] Such people don't come to Christ for help because they don't see their need.

In contrast, people like the woman in Solomon's court know they need mercy. The Prodigal Son knows it. The tax collector who prays, "God, be merciful to me, a sinner!" knows it. And the woman who is forgiven after washing Jesus' feet with her tears knows it. They receive mercy from God because they boldly come and ask him for it. Though

[5] Luke 15:11-31.
[6] Luke 18:11-12.
[7] Luke 7:36-50.

they know they don't deserve it, those who know their need and come to God get mercy and kindness.

A MODERN PROSTITUTE

Growing up, one of my favorite comic books retold the story of Howard Rutledge, a Vietnam prisoner of war who entitled his autobiography, *In the Presence of Mine Enemies: 1965-1973*. Captain Rutledge was a man with no right to expect God to care about him. He had been given more than his share of the best opportunities in life: a healthy upbringing, a good career, and a loving family. Nevertheless, he squandered those good things by ignoring the God who gave them.

He had walked in the ways of Deuteronomy 8, forgetting that the good things he had were gifts direct from God's hand. He slowly lost interest in his Creator and prized his career over his relationship with his God. Such a man has no right to expect help from God in times of trouble. He should expect to reap what he has sown.

While serving in Vietnam, Rutledge was shot down and confined for eight years in various prison camps. Malnutrition, isolation, and torture were the mainstays of his life, and in his misery he cried out to God. He had ignored God, but God refused to ignore him. Instead, God drew near by his Spirit, and turned Rutledge's soul around. The Lord strengthened him to endure weeks of torture and years of isolation and deprivation. God taught him about himself by bringing Bible passages and hymns to his mind and instructing him through other prisoners. Eventually God did release him from the camp, but more than that, he released him from an eternal prison.

Two people: Rutledge and a nameless prostitute. Both shared the sin of spiritual prostitution, but they also shared a God who did not give them what they deserved, withholding himself from them. He answered their cries for help.

No matter where your own spiritual unfaithfulness has taken you, you also can experience a God who will treat you better than you deserve. God showcases the prostitute's story to increase your confidence that he will receive you too, regardless of your history or baggage. All you need is to come to him with hope that he will hear and act on your behalf. Though you are convicted of your unworthiness, come to him, convinced that he will help.

on your own

1   The prostitute's tale may still strike you as an odd story, so think about it from God's perspective. If you only saw God's wisdom displayed in the lives of worthy people, how would your faith suffer?

2   In what ways do you have difficulty identifying with the prostitute? Do you see equally your need for God's mercy and his willingness to give it?

3   What keeps you from boldly hoping that God desires to help you? After hearing this story, hopelessness should be all but banished, yet in some hearts it remains stubbornly entrenched. If that is true of you, ask yourself why hopelessness is more appealing than hope. What keeps you from wanting God's mercy? What do you get out of believing that God could never receive you?

4   Other people struggle more with arrogance than with hopelessness. What kinds of people or sins are easy for you to look down on? Where do you lack sympathy, patience, or understanding? What types of people bring out the "older brother" in you? Does it upset you when God is kind to them? Does mercy grip you as strongly as justice?

Are you worried he won't help you until your faith gets stronger?

The story of the prostitute emphasizes that God rewards those who come to him with confidence. You have to believe that he will receive you and treat you well. But isn't that part of the problem? Hebrews 11:6 declares that without faith we cannot hope to please God, and for some that feels like an impossible hurdle – like you don't have enough cash for the entrance fee. Ask yourself, *How confident am I that God will treat me well?* For many, answering this question reveals the unbelief mixed in with their faith. We do believe Jesus, yet we also struggle to believe him. What are you supposed to do if your hope in God's goodness is feeble and frail?

It almost starts to sound as if Scripture advocates taking a "blind leap" in order to know God better. One day, you should just decide to trust God and hope for the best, not because there's any reason to do so, but because that's what you're supposed to do. That might work with people who are fairly self-confident, but not many timid people are capable of it.

Scripture, however, describes an entirely different dynamic. In the Bible, God shows you how he has worked with other people who have had similar doubts and reservations. Instead of taking blind leaps of faith, God wants you to develop an informed confidence in his character. Scripture demonstrates how God deals with people who don't fully trust him so that you can understand how Jesus will handle your weak faith once he seeks you out and finds you.

An Unlikely Warrior

As my family read the story of Gideon together,[1] we were struck by his timidity. We first encounter Gideon hiding in a winepress, threshing out his wheat so that the Midianites won't steal it. Skulking and deception are not an auspicious introduction to a future deliverer of Israel!

Then God addresses him: "The LORD is with you, mighty warrior."[2] Gideon seems as surprised as we are. Can you hear him thinking, *Are you kidding? Look at me! I'm hiding in a winepress!* God chose that less-than-courageous circumstance to tell Gideon that he would save Israel. Have you noticed how often God says things that defy all of our circumstances and experiences?

Gideon, unconvinced, asks for a sign to assure him that God is truly speaking to him. He asks if the angel of the Lord would stay for a meal as proof. God agrees and Gideon leaves to prepare a young goat and unleavened bread. Imagine God waiting around while Gideon cooks! He had a golden opportunity to depart, should God want to rethink his choice of a deliverer. But the Lord graciously stays until Gideon returns. He knows how difficult this calling is for Gideon, so he waits patiently to bolster his faith.

As you may know, this first sign wasn't enough for Gideon and he later asks for more proof.[3] For his second test, he asks God to wet a fleece but not the ground around it. God complies. Then Gideon wants the fleece dry and the surrounding ground wet. That was the third sign he asked for and, again, God provides it. But don't miss the point of the story. The Bible is not developing a theology of setting out fleeces to determine God's will. Rather, God wants you to see the weakness of his chosen vessel and, more importantly, his kind concern in the face of Gideon's lingering doubt and unbelief.

On the eve of battle with the Midianites, Gideon is still nervous, but this time he doesn't get the chance to ask for a sign. God takes the initiative and offers him one more.[4] God tells him that if he's still afraid, he should go down to the enemy camp and listen to the soldiers talk among themselves. Gideon listens to two guards discussing a dream and overhears them interpret it to mean that Gideon would destroy them all!

It is amazing to see how God anticipated Gideon's faith battle and built his confidence by infiltrating the minds of his enemies. Gideon could no longer doubt his future victory when he has heard the enemy

[1] Judg. 6-8.
[2] Judg. 6:12.
[3] Judg. 6:36-39.
[4] Judg. 7:9-15.

prophesy their own defeat. Again, notice how God interacts with Gideon. He doesn't berate him for his lack of faith. Instead, he stoops even lower to give him the faith to believe. Gideon's need for such encouragement remains a constant throughout his story, and God keeps intensifying his responses. He goes from patiently waiting for Gideon's return, to actively altering the physical world, to proactively initiating the last sign.

Gideon was not a brave man, but that didn't keep God from using him. He took the man he wanted, warts and all, and delivered Israel from her enemies by his hand. He used his chosen vessel despite that vessel's repeated struggle to trust what God had told him.

AN EVEN MORE UNLIKELY FATHER

Another case where you see God's concern for his doubting children is with Abraham. *Abraham? I thought he was the man who believed God and had it credited to him as righteousness!*[5]

We're talking about the same guy. Genesis 15 tells us that Abraham believed that God would give him a son – he had faith – and God credited his faith as the kind of righteousness he desired. And yet, as Abraham continued speaking with God, you realize that his faith was not as strong as it could have been. God promised to give him the land he was standing on and Abraham responded, "O Sovereign LORD, how can I know that I will gain possession of it?"[6] This is a statement of faith in that he is talking to God. It's not outright unbelief. But it's not complete confidence either, seeing that he is asking for something to back up God's words.

God responds by making his covenant with Abraham, an intensely meaningful ceremony that remains difficult for us in the modern world to grasp. He didn't merely make a verbal promise; his presence passed between two rows of cut-up animals. In this vivid picture, God swore to carry out his promise or be sliced in two, just like the sacrifices.[7] He answered Abraham's fears and faith struggles by basing his promise on his own faithfulness.

Abraham needed that covenant because not only did he struggle with believing God, he also struggled with obeying him. Immediately after this promise and sign, Abraham slept with Sarah's maid to generate an heir.[8] A few chapters later, he lied, saying that Sarah was his sister to

---

5 Gen. 15:6.
6 Gen. 15:8.
7 Gen. 15:17.
8 Gen. 16:3-4.

avoid being killed.[9] If Abraham was worried about living to see the end of the day, he couldn't have had much confidence that he would inherit any land. Weak faith and blatant sin both lived in this man of faith.

Imagine you are Abraham after such a lapse. What do you hold onto if you've just lied about your wife . . . again? Does your faithlessness nullify the promises God made to you? Does your faithlessness cancel out the faith you had earlier so that God now credits it to you as unrighteousness?

What about the fiasco with Ishmael? Do you wander outside at night, looking at the stars as you sigh, "As many as the stars . . . . Will it still happen . . . or have I ruined everything?" Do you wonder if the promised child is no longer promised? How about five years later when there is still no Isaac? How about ten? Are you tempted as the years roll by to hope for less than what God had promised? If you were Abraham and tempted to lose hope, you also might think back to the covenant God made with you; that time when you were weak in faith and needed him to strengthen you . . . and he did.

Abraham's faith was not perfect – far from it. But the covenant was never based on his perfection. It was based on God and God's perfection. Abraham's faith believed that God would do what he said, despite his own human failings. This is our hope too. It's the confidence Paul expresses when he quotes, "If we are faithless, he will remain faithful, for he cannot disown himself."[10]

WHAT HOLDS YOU BACK?

Not trusting God is cosmic insanity. On what basis did Abraham and Gideon doubt him? For that matter, on what basis do you and I doubt him? He's the one person whose love, care, and sacrifice have been constant in our lives.

It's a little like when I tell my children, "No, you cannot have a cookie right now," and they walk away frowning and grumbling. Granted, I am not the best parent on earth, but I try to do what is best for them. I am not capricious or unconcerned regarding what they would like, and I am not intentionally mean to them. Furthermore, I have done many good things for them that they would acknowledge if they thought about it. Yet they do not always believe that I have their best interests at heart. That's true insanity: when you choose to believe relational fantasy over

---

[9] Gen. 20:1-2.
[10] 2 Tim. 2:13.

reality simply because you didn't get what you wanted. And yet I act the same way toward God with even less justification. He would increase my faith and yours if we would let him. But perhaps the hard truth is that we just don't want more faith to trust him.

My friend Amy didn't want to come nearer to God because she was afraid he wouldn't reciprocate. Insanity? Yes, but with a compelling logic. She feared that if she approached him, he wouldn't want her and wouldn't respond to her. "And if that happened," she said, "where would I be? I would have gambled everything, leaving myself no backup plan, and wound up with nothing! But if I don't move toward him, even though I have a weak relationship with him, I can at least tell myself that I could if I wanted to." Amy consoled herself with the thought that life could always be better, but if she reached toward God and he didn't respond, she'd have nothing to fall back on. She existed on her dreams of what life could be while denying herself the reality. Avoiding greater faith made sense to her. She eliminated the risk, but she also eliminated the relationship. Sometimes weak faith speaks with a fearful voice.

At other times, weak faith speaks out of ignorance. We want more faith, but won't ask because we feel as though we don't deserve it. We don't fully believe God is close to us. We struggle to believe he'll watch our back or that he'll never leave us or forsake us. And so we conclude, ignorantly, that because we have little faith, we have no basis for asking for more. Surprisingly, these weak moments are precisely when faith can be most alive. Remember how Jesus welcomed weary souls to come to him for rest? How, instead of scolding weak people, he encouraged them to believe that his Father would give the Holy Spirit to any who asked?

When our weak faith hinders us from approaching Christ, we've actually misunderstood faith's essence. Faith is not a feeling of being spiritually strong or superior, either in our relationship with Christ or in our activities. Such feelings can have very little to do with faith. Rather, faith is the confidence that God will receive you even when you're not put together very well. Strong faith doesn't mean you walk effortlessly through life. It means you run quickly to Christ when you're in need.

There's a very small – almost imperceptible – gap between weak faith that speaks ignorantly and weak faith that speaks arrogantly. Some people don't approach Christ for more faith because they prefer to limp along without him. They would rather rely on five communication principles for mistake-proof conversations than trust the One who made their mouths to fill them with his words. Other people want to feel energized at the end of a long, hard day of housecleaning; they don't want to ask Jesus simply for the strength to begin the next room. Gideon couldn't carry out his mission without constant reliance on God, but too many of us want to fulfill our mission without him. Relying on Christ doesn't look attractive, and it doesn't feel strong.

Unfortunately, such proud self-reliance is common to us all. There is little that our sinful humanity fights harder than an active, regular, prolonged dependence on Christ to handle the difficulties of daily life. All of us know the part of our soul that rejects depending on him to live a life that pleases him. Reversing John 15, deep down we prefer to believe that we, the branches, can do things of eternal worth and value apart from Christ, the Vine. And so we don't come to him, asking him for greater faith.

FAITHFUL TO THE FAITHLESS

And yet, despite it all, God is kind to people who shrink back from trusting him. There's a special place in his heart for those with little faith. Jesus still invites you to say to him, along with the father of the epileptic boy, "I do believe; help me overcome my unbelief!"[11]

Your first step simply involves asking for help. Both Abraham and Gideon took their lack of faith to the Source of faith. Begin there yourself. Acknowledge your difficulty in trusting him; admit that you need his help to believe him. Trust him to handle you as patiently as he did your weak brothers in the Bible.

Second, take a moment to consider where you've seen your God (unnecessarily) prove his reliability to you. Remember when you first came to him and he received you. Or cast your mind back to that sin you carried around for months, afraid to admit it to yourself, much less to him. Remember how he flooded you with forgiveness and relief? You weren't sure he'd receive you, yet he did. Take a moment to review the ways he has already handled your moments of weak faith.

Last, you need to act on the faith God gives you. When some people hear how much God does to change people, they wrongly believe that they contribute nothing to their own lives. This is almost as dangerous as thinking you don't need Christ at all! Living passively saps your will and cripples your belief that you can accomplish what God calls you to do. Living faithfully means that you actively respond to the faith God gives you.

---

[11] Mark 9:24.

When my daughter was two, she was uninterested in eating. We would pray with her, asking Jesus to help her want to eat, but then we would also ask, "Do you think God is going to come down now, pick up your fork, and shovel dinner into your mouth?" Giggling, she'd roll her eyes and say, "No!" We would then say, "You're right! But he will change you inside to want to eat. And now you have to respond by picking up your fork."

The same is true for me and you. Jesus wants us to live a faithful life that relies on him. He rebuked the disciples several times for their lack of faith, but in a way that pointed them back to him as the Source of faith. If your faith is small because of fearfulness, ignorance, or arrogance, ask him to increase your faith so that you can carry out his desires faithfully. Along with Augustine, pray, "Grant what you command and command what you will." Entrust him with your weak faith; he longs to supply what you lack.

1   Where in your life do you currently have trouble believing God? What has he given you to do that exceeds your abilities?

2   When you struggle with weak faith, does it tend to be out of fearfulness, ignorance, or arrogance? Having a better sense of the kind of weakness you struggle with gives you a clearer idea of how your faith needs to grow. Make sure you ask the Lord to forgive you before moving on.

3   Think carefully: What has Jesus done in the past when you struggled to believe him? How has he increased your faith? Thank him for his past kindnesses and for reminding you how he's been active. Ask him to strengthen your faith now.

4   Think carefully again: what small step do you need to take today to put faith into action? Take that step and allow yourself to be amazed at how God is working in you.

Are you scared he'll reject you when you let him down?

Sometimes weak faith looks like nervousness or uncertainty. Those are times when you're not sure if God is big enough to take care of you. Then there are the times when you are certain that he's not. At those times you act faithlessly by running from what he's called you to do. Even then, God draws near to restore you so that you can live faithfully again.

Do you remember jerking awake as a child with your chest pounding? You had just had that dream and its remnants still clutched at your mind. Fear – even terror – are words too tame to describe what you felt as you huddled under your covers. What could be worse? But there was something worse: that long walk down the hall to your parents' room for comfort.

What gave you the courage to get up and get started? Only your confidence that someone at the other end of that hallway would welcome you and set the world right. If all you had was the certainty of ridicule or rejection, you would not bother to go. You might have had parents who were big enough to handle your fright, but they weren't kind enough. Facing them would be even scarier than braving the dark hallway! Or you might have had kind parents, but you didn't believe they were strong enough to provide the comfort you sought. You actually felt safer dealing with your panic alone. But if you knew that someone could and would help you, somehow you would put feet to faith and make your way – inching (or sprinting!) – down the hall.

Elijah was the sprinting sort – but initially his running had nothing to do with confidently seeking help. In 1 Kings 18:16-19:3 he had just presided over a compelling demonstration of God's power and Baal's impotency on Mount Carmel. He had called the Israelite nation to witness the confrontation between himself, God's sole representative, and Baal's 450 prophets. Both sides constructed altars with unlit sacrifices and then called on their god to send fire from heaven. Baal did not answer, but the God of Israel did – burning up not only the sacrifice but the stones as well, along with the water that drenched the entire altar. Clearly, powerfully, and decisively, the Lord showed that he was God and Baal was not. Elijah then oversaw the slaughter of the false prophets who had led Israel dangerously astray. Surely, after such an awesome display, Elijah would have had even more confidence in his God. Right? Wrong. Immediately afterward, Queen Jezebel threatened to kill Elijah. In response he fled into the desert, praying that he might die.

On the Lam

It's surprising that Elijah ran when he did. Clearly, he was a man of courage and conviction to be able to stand alone, unwavering, in front of an agnostic crowd, against religious opponents who were backed by royal wealth and power. You would think that if he were to run, it would be before God demonstrated his power, not after. Was Elijah's U-turn the result of emotional exhaustion after the day-long confrontation? Had he suffered a mild nervous breakdown, having reached the limit of his internal resources? As interesting as such speculations may be, Scripture doesn't explore his mental distress. It chooses instead to focus on the fact that he abandoned the job God gave him to do as Israel's prophet. And Elijah agreed with that assessment. He admitted that he had wrongly given up as he prayed in the desert, "Take my life; I am no better than my ancestors."[1]

When we lose confidence in God, we never do so in the abstract. Rather, our faith dissolves in concrete situations where God doesn't seem up to the job. Elijah's situation involved a very scary woman. When she threatened him he ran, revealing his false faith that she could affect his life more than the Lord. And yet, Elijah felt conviction of sin. He knew he'd sold God out, hence his conclusion that he was no better than anyone else. Life had become a messy, vicious cycle that made it hard even to consider approaching people again. Look at the nasty tangle in Elijah's life:

- fear experienced on a horizontal plane (regarding Jezebel)
- triggers vertical faith loss (regarding the Lord)
- resulting in internal recriminations (against himself).

---

[1] 1 Kings 19:4.

Have you ever wanted to run because you "knew" God wasn't big enough to handle what you were facing? Often that feeling accompanies the belief that other people are functionally more powerful than God – that they can disrupt our lives more than he can redeem them. I regularly face this temptation with pushy, strong-willed people, especially the prickly and hypersensitive variety. I am tempted to back down from such people and pull my punches. I don't believe that God's promise to be with me is enough for such a difficult encounter. And I am not alone.

Have you ever received a phone call you didn't want to return? Or put off a confrontation because you knew nothing good would come of it? Have you ever hidden your faith in Christ in a potentially hostile environment – school classroom, business ethics seminar, neighborhood party? There are many ways to avoid what God has given you to do because you don't believe he is up to the challenge. You do this despite the way God has helped you in the past and proven himself faithful. Refusing the Lord's call and running from scary people is a very human experience. Fortunately, dealing well with frightened people is one of God's specialties.

NOT TOO BIG TO BE GENTLE

Think about this story from God's perspective. He had already demonstrated his commitment to Elijah's welfare by feeding him during a three-year drought[2] and vindicating him completely at the top of Mount Carmel, making every word Elijah said come true. Elijah had no reason to believe God could not handle Jezebel, but still Elijah ran.

Here's a place where it would make sense for God to hand Elijah a pink slip: "Okay, you just blew it! I show everyone my power and glory, and you, my servant, turn around and show everyone you don't really believe I'm equal to the challenge. I need someone who shows others what confident faith looks like. Clean out your desk; I'm through with you!"

Remarkably, God did not ridicule or berate him. Nor did he reject him and find someone else to complete the mission. Instead, when Elijah arrived in the desert, God sent an angel to feed and strengthen him.[3] Not only did Elijah's strength revive, so did his faith. Instead of simply running away from the enemy, he ran toward his Lord. Elijah may not have had enough faith to face the queen he had angered, but he learned he could face the God he had failed.

---

[2] 1 Kings 17:1-16.
[3] 1 Kings 19:5-8.

He went to the mountain where God met his people when they came out of Egypt. There God came to him and asked, "What are you doing here, Elijah?"4 Doesn't that amaze you? Elijah has dropped the ball horribly, yet God moves toward him to start a conversation! And look at his opening. He doesn't begin by rebuking him, telling him that he shouldn't be scared or that he had no reason to feel the way he did. Instead, he invites Elijah to talk about why he ran away. God begins by focusing on his servant, not his servant's failings.

As Elijah talked, his warped thinking came to the surface. He described all the mighty people stacked against him. He portrayed himself as the lone champion, relegating God to the role of disinterested bystander. When Elijah tells the story, God merely serves as the backdrop for the real action of everyone ganging up on a defenseless individual. Elijah seemed to have forgotten the power God had so vividly displayed against the servants of Baal only forty days earlier.

But instead of correcting Elijah or defending himself, God invited Elijah to another demonstration of power. He sent a mighty wind, an earthquake, a fire, and then finally, in a whisper, his own voice.5 Do you have the picture? God could easily have given a three-part sermon on how his power stacks up against any human sovereign's. Instead he chose to show Elijah that, compared to him, Jezebel's power was pitiful. As long as Elijah saw Jezebel as the biggest player on the stage, it made sense to run from her. Therefore, God put things in a bigger perspective, where Elijah could see that she was not even in the same league as the Lord. Elijah needed to experience this difference to have any hope of reordering his perspective.

Yet God did not inhabit the frightening things he brought – the wind, earthquake, and fire. He made a very clear distinction between his potential power and his actual interactions with his servant. Throughout the rest of the story, God continued to be kind and gentle. Here's a God big enough to handle the things that terrify his people yet kind enough not to terrorize them. He is a God who later comes in human form to fulfill the prophecy, "A bruised reed he will not break, and a smoldering wick he will not snuff out."6

And Elijah was bruised. That fact can be so easy to miss when someone has let you down. Sadly, I find it all too easy to overlook the person and focus on how the unfinished task complicates my life. In those

---

4 1 Kings 19:9.
5 1 Kings 19:11-13.
6 Matt. 12:20.

moments I prize the work over the worker. And then I get irritated. God responded differently because he cared more for Elijah than he cared for his performance. Elijah's false belief in God's smallness had paralyzed him, making him unable to function in God's kingdom. Rather than discarding him, God sought to reorient Elijah's faith so that he could resume the work he had been given. For God, his purposes are important and they will be fulfilled, but not at the expense of his people. He brings about his plans in a way that also restores the children he loves.

Having displayed his power and his tenderness, God again asks, "What are you doing here, Elijah?"[7] Again Elijah recites his faithless litany of complaints, word for word as he did earlier. Even at this point, when his attempt to reorient Elijah has seemingly failed, God does not throw up his hands in despair and walk away. He understood that Elijah needed a new focus, so he gave him very clear instructions on what to do next.[8] Among other things, those instructions would lead to Jezebel's removal from power. It's tempting to believe God did this so that Elijah could breathe more easily. But that would be to misunderstand God's purposes. Jezebel needed to be removed primarily because she was obstructing God's plan and God still wanted Elijah involved in bringing it about.

What God did do just for Elijah's benefit was to let him in on a secret:[9] he was not alone in his devotion to God. God let Elijah know that he had seven thousand friends he knew nothing about! Fear isolates because it lies. You cannot always expect God to remove the source of your greatest fears, but you can be certain that he will reconnect you with his community and get you back in step with his kingdom plans.

KNOWINGLY UNASHAMED

It is amazing to realize that God does not hold even your unreasonable fearfulness against you. When it manifests itself in missed evangelistic moments, paralysis during peacemaking, and cowardly confrontations, we feel ashamed and wrongly conclude that God must be even more ashamed of us. We know what it is to pray with Elijah, "I am no better than my ancestors."

Rick knew firsthand what it was to run from God's call. He had taken on more than he could handle. His wife had agreed that he should quit his successful job, sell their house, and move their family so that he could study for the ministry. In light of these sacrifices, Rick desperately

---

[7] 1 Kings 19:13.
[8] 1 Kings 19:15-18.
[9] 1 Kings 19:18.

longed to succeed in his studies to prove that they had made the right decisions. He also felt the need to support his family financially, but his meager income didn't come close to meeting their weekly expenses. As they slipped deeper and deeper into debt, he worked harder, but his studies suffered and so did his family relationships.

Rick broke under the strain. When we first met, he was severely depressed. The need to succeed at school had captured all his attention, pushing out any sense of God's presence, call, or purpose in his life. However, he hadn't been able to finish the semester and he was planning to take a leave of absence from the next. No longer able to succeed, his life's purpose seemed to evaporate. Daily he contemplated the "disaster" and "ruin" of his life, further isolating himself from his family. His wife felt she had lost her husband's company along with everything else. But Rick was too ashamed of himself to believe his wife wasn't ashamed as well. He could not imagine how he could make things up to her. Without literally abandoning his wife, his fear and shame drove him to withdraw internally, creating miles of emotional distance at a time when they desperately needed each other. Rick's failure fueled his avoidance and perpetuated this destructive relational cycle.

Though Rick and Elijah's situations are very different, you can see in both the deadly intersection between making something larger than God, the isolation and tangled human relationships that result, and our own sense of shame at not living up to our calling. I thought it might be profitable one day to begin with Rick as God did with Elijah, by suggesting that God was better than Rick dared to believe. We turned to that amazing passage in Hebrews where we are told that "Jesus is not ashamed to call them brothers."[10] We saw that Jesus is referring to fellow sufferers, like Rick himself, who are tempted to sin.[11] We realized that Jesus doesn't turn away from Rick; instead he points him out and says, "Do you see Rick there? He's my brother! I am not ashamed of him." Rick's eyes slowly filled with tears. He'd thought it impossible for anyone not to be ashamed of him after he had let everyone down, especially the Lord who had called him to this work. Yet there it was, in black and white: Jesus is not ashamed to call him his brother.

---

[10] Heb. 2:10-11.

[11] Larger context of Hebrews 2, especially vv. 14-18. F. F. Bruce in *The Epistle to the Hebrews*, Revised Edition (Grand Rapids: William B. Eerdmans Publishing Company, 1990) more explicitly highlights Jesus' positive attitude toward his people despite their horrible failings when he notes that these people of whom Jesus is not ashamed are also those ". . . for whose sins he made atonement, that they might follow him to glory on the path of salvation which he himself cut" (p. 81).

To believe that Jesus was not ashamed of him meant that Rick had to accept God's appraisal of his life over his own assessment. Believing that Jesus accepted him despite his failures gave Rick the security he needed to see where the semester had gone wrong and why he had not sought help earlier. It challenged his assumption that he was only worthwhile if he was successful. Jesus' acceptance allowed him to begin rejoining his family as a valued and contributing member – not on the strength of his own accomplishments, but on God's.

Rick's hope grew when he saw that God had not given up on him. People who feel like quitting need to be surprised by a God who never does.

on your own

1   Where do you feel you've let God down? What things have you attempted
    for God, only to abandon because they felt too big? Where do you feel
    ashamed before God?

2   Sometimes we rightly feel shame for things that should embarrass us; at
    other times we're wrongly ashamed of things that aren't our fault. In
    either case, the cure is the same: to realize that Jesus is not ashamed to
    own you as part of his family. Meditate on the fact that Christ is not
    ashamed of you! Allow the reality of your gracious God to sink deeply
    into your soul.

3   What will you need to let go of to enter into God's acceptance? Said dif-
    ferently, what will it cost you to agree with Jesus? This is another good
    place to repent for overvaluing your own opinions (or others') over God's.

4   Where have you experienced the combination of God's greatness and
    gentleness? Ask friends for their stories: how has God subdued their
    fears by dealing gently with them?

Part III

God provides
what you need

We've looked at God's heart for his lost sheep and considered some of the misconceptions those sheep have about him. In this part, we will examine certain ways God helps his people to move forward. Too often we look at our failings and wrongly conclude that holiness and a good relationship with Jesus are simply not possible. We quit before we start. We discredit God's promise to help us live lives that glorify him. We also overlook the many resources he gives us so that we can honor him in difficult times. The following chapters illustrate the ways God will help you as you seek to live a righteous life.

Do you seize the chances Jesus gives you?

Out of his kindness, God often gives us another chance to turn to him for mercy. Nina, however, like too many of us, repeatedly rejected such offers. She grew up gladly participating in church-related activities, but in her teens she began to struggle with how faith would fit into her life. She discovered that some of the most religious-sounding kids in her youth group lived hypocritically. Their religious talk and activities led people to believe that they were actually spiritual. Hypocrisy notwithstanding, they belonged to the in-crowd – "cool" kids who attracted her but who had questionable faith. Nina compared her church friends with people at school whose religious lifestyles made them look strange to her. These kids had faith but seemed either "geeky" or immature. Allured by popularity and repulsed by weirdness, Nina's potential faith was soon stifled.

At college a classmate witnessed to her. Despite her ability to give him the "right" answers, Nina realized she didn't know if she was going to heaven. She pursued her friend with questions that he answered well, but eventually Nina told him, "I believe it's all true, but I just don't want it." Fun and the approval of her friends had won her heart. She asked him, "Please don't talk to me about these things anymore," as she gave herself to friends, parties, and travel.

AIMING FOR THE FENCE

Every Christian has been Nina at some point in his or her life; there have been times when we've all stiff-armed the Lord, preferring to go our own way. We have defiantly parodied Christ by telling him, "Not your will, but mine be done." Not every rebellious story goes on for years; some last only months or weeks. Nor are such stories limited to the time before we came to know Christ. Each one of us has knowingly resisted the Lord at some point in his or her Christian life. Maybe you are at that point right now.

Can you think back to a time when, as a Christian, you found yourself planning to give in to sin? You started toying with the idea days in advance, fantasizing about what you were going to do. You turned memories over in your mind, tasting the bitter sweetness of the guilty past, fueling your present desire, and fixing your determination to experience it again. Sure, you put up a feeble resistance by rehearsing limits and boundaries to prevent gross sin, but your ideas ran as close as possible to those limits. In those moments you replaced *How holy can I be?* with *How far can I go?* or *How much will God let me get away with?*

Picture a pasture encircled by a protective fence with a shepherd at its center. Are you a sheep who typically moves toward the center, longing to be with your shepherd? Or are you more likely to be hugging the fence, hungering for what's on the other side? This is the difference between a life that presses the limits of Christian propriety and a life that longs to be near Jesus. Which way are you pointed? When you always head toward the fence, you will eventually cross it, first in your worship and then with your body. Nina struck out for the fence and rejected the shepherd, first with her heart and then with her life. Her story is not so different from that of Ahab, one of Israel's worst kings.

Elected to the Hall of Shame

When we want to assess those currently in power, we often compare them to prominent figures from the past, people who rose above the crowd like Churchill, Hitler, and Stalin. We then use these people as standards against which we compare someone new. In the process, they lose their unique, individual personalities and become archetypes for good or evil.

The author of 1 Kings does the same thing. When he wants to draw your attention to someone's goodness, he references King David and the ways in which David led Israel to follow the Lord. When he wants to alert you that a king was evil, he likens him to King Jeroboam, who set the pace and trajectory for idolatry in Israel. Strikingly, however, the author introduces a second exemplar for evil midway through his narrative – Ahab.

Ahab, we are told, not only walked in the sins of Jeroboam, he exceeded them.[1] Through his wife Jezebel's influence, he legitimized Baal worship in Israel and approved the persecution of those who worshiped God, leaving prophets the choice to hide or die. As we read earlier, Elijah thought he was the last prophet to remain faithful to Jehovah during Ahab's regime. Ahab rejected all he knew of God and pursued his own course. The author not only compares later unrighteous kings to Jeroboam but also invokes Ahab to emphasize how evil they were.[2] Although one of Israel's mightiest kings, you wouldn't name your son after him.

Being the worst of the worst has a perverse kind of status to it. Ahab's notoriety is noteworthy, but what's more striking is how much God extended himself to this king who worked so hard to ruin Israel. God literally went out of his way to get Ahab's attention. He withheld rain from the land to convince Ahab that his course was destructive, both to himself and the nation. God crushed Baal's prophets, demonstrating his power and superiority through a sign unlike any other. He then provided rain, showing that his kindness was still available even though Ahab had not yet repented. He even rescued Israel, still ruled by Ahab – twice – from a coalition of nations that should have crushed the little kingdom. God warned, disciplined, and showered kindness on a man who did not deserve God's continued involvement in his life. Yet Ahab kept going his own way, setting his heart against his Creator, and allowing evil to rule God's people.

You learn something about hard hearts from Ahab. You learn how easy it is to overlook God's attempts to get your attention. You learn how easy it is to ignore God to your own detriment. You learn how a foolish, darkened heart blinds you to the true meaning and implications of your actions. But even more illuminating than Ahab's commitment to evil is God's commitment to Ahab. Despite Ahab's repeated rebuffs, God continued his efforts to gain his rebellious creature's attention. He used his power to give Ahab multiple chances, choosing not to destroy him. He yearned for Ahab to see his evil and turn from it. But for how long?

After numerous rejections, I would think it was time to give up. What more could God do? He would have been fully justified not to give Ahab any more chances to repent. Why not let Ahab reap all he had sown? But God, who is better than I can imagine, was not finished.

---

[1] 1 Kings 16:30.
[2] See, for instance, 1 Kings 22:52; 2 Kings 3:2; 8:18, 25-27; and 21:3.

HOUNDED

Ahab sinned again. He allowed a righteous man, Naboth, to be murdered so that he could turn Naboth's family's inheritance into a vegetable garden near his palace.[3] There are no limits we won't cross when we harden our hearts against God! But watch God swing into action. This last sin of Ahab's was relatively small compared to all the other lives he had helped ruin, but it was not too small for God to overlook. God sent Elijah to confront him one more time, this time with the doom of the Lord. And hardened old Ahab repented!

He tore his clothes, put on sackcloth, fasted, and was dejected. Incredible! After all he had done and all the chances God had given him, Ahab finally got it. He opened his eyes and saw the world the way God saw it. He turned back from where he was going. And God, who knows our hearts, declared that Ahab's repentance was genuine. He had truly humbled himself and God relented from his plans to destroy Ahab.

It's amazing that a man could change like that but more amazing that our God would give him that one extra chance. It would have been so easy for God not to warn him and simply destroy Ahab and his family. Warning him involved much more effort. God had to send Elijah to speak to a man who had been completely uninterested in anything God had to say. God took the time and trouble because that's his nature. He pursues people – even hardened, fist-in-his-face people – to give them the opportunity to repent.

Six years after her eyes-wide-open rejection of God, Nina repented. She had lived those years with a deep awareness of God pursuing her. Her Christian friend's words reverberated in her head, reminding her of the implications of the short-sighted choices she continued to make. Scripture they had studied together, especially passages portraying God as a loving father, kept coming to her mind. Little things that other people might dismiss as mere coincidence – accidentally tuning in to a Billy Graham crusade on TV or discovering a Christian tract – communicated loudly that God was not about to let her run from him.

Less pleasant experiences also drove her back to God. As she reeled drunkenly across a street one night, narrowly missed by an oncoming car, she thought, *Nina, you are playing Russian roulette with your soul!* Jesus combined these experiences to produce an inner wrestling in which he finally prevailed.

---

3 1 Kings 21:1-29.

When God sent her yet another invitation to a Bible study, Nina recognized the voice of her Shepherd. This time she did not refuse his summons. On her way to the study, she burst into tears and prayed in her car, "If you love me enough to pursue me after six years, then this time, I'm not saying 'no'." Her heart changed at that moment. God's goodness and mercy stood out against her earlier vehement "no." In her words, she "never turned back after that night."

In his poem, "The Hound of Heaven," Francis Thompson describes a man's (perhaps his own?) experience of running from God. Although this man desired many things apart from Christ and wanted nothing to do with him, Christ pursued him. Three times Thompson closes an account of the struggling man's experience with a refrain that details God's pursuit even as he tries to run and hide.

> But with unhurrying chase,
> And unperturbéd pace,
> Deliberate speed, majestic instancy,
> They beat – and a Voice beat
> More instant than the Feet –

Each time the Voice speaks, it tries to educate the man as to why all his attempts at living life end so vainly and unsatisfactorily.

The Voice explains how God himself has pulled the rug out from under the man so that he will not eternally destroy himself. After those three sections, the man appears to stop running and reflect on his ruined life, at which point the Voice surrounds him. It reaffirms that though the man cannot expect to find love and comfort anywhere on earth, given all that he is and has done, the Voice will still love and receive him. Never frantic. Never letting up. Never giving up.

Surely Thompson understood something of human nature that instinctively flees from God and tries to use his world against him. But he also understood something of God's pursuit of fleeing humanity. This pursuit humbles me. Given the terribly small number of chances I give people, I am simply amazed at what I learn from Ahab, Nina, and my own experience. I encounter a God who truly does not delight in the death of the wicked but rather offers them many opportunities to turn.

NEITHER UNLIMITED NOR UNCONDITIONAL

It's not just the outrageously wicked who need multiple chances. Many people in church resist God's Spirit as well. They pretend that his words don't apply to them or their situation. They tell themselves that their disobedience won't impact the rest of their lives, so they can safely ignore his prodding. In response to their hard hearts, Jesus continues calling them through sermons, his Word, his Spirit, and his people. He warns them. He showers them with kindness. He gives chance after chance to repent. Unfortunately, there are those who remain as indifferent to these opportunities as Ahab was for most of his life.

Do you see parallels in your life? Do you care little for God's efforts to bring you back to himself, shrugging them off as you keep doing the things you prefer? Yes, God gives you opportunities to turn to him, but please don't believe that he obligates himself to do so indefinitely. I am always sobered when I consider Cain. When Cain slaughtered his brother Abel, God had already pursued him, warning him not to give in to sin.[4] After the murder, God gave him the same chance he had given his father Adam – the chance to confess what he had done. But Cain arrogantly threw the opportunity back in God's face by sarcastically asking, "Am I my brother's keeper?" God responded by banishing him, closing Cain's window of opportunity. God gives opportunities, but he expects us to respond to them. For those who refuse his mercy, only judgment remains.

The Israelites repeatedly tried and tested God in the desert, attributing all sorts of evil motives and intentions to him, saying that he was only interested in killing them by thirst, hunger, or enemies. Over and over in the books of Exodus and Numbers, you see a patient God restrain himself from destroying his people. He provides for them, gives them signs, and disciplines them, yet they refuse to trust him. When they reach the edge of the Promised Land, the spies' report leads them to again charge that God is planning to kill them. At this point, God said, "Enough!" He sentenced them to wander in the desert (because they were not free to return to Egypt) and die (because they were no longer free to enter Canaan). He withdrew the opportunity to possess the land when they refused to respond with faith.

Ahab and Nina had no idea what a fine razor's edge they were blundering along. All too often I don't either. How about you? How many times have you heard someone say – or said yourself, "I know what I'm

---

4 Gen. 4:6-7.

doing is wrong, but I'm going to do it anyway. Later on God will forgive me"? I cringe when I hear that. Don't we understand how presumptuous we are to think that, after hardening our hearts, we'll be *able* to repent again? When God offers you the chance to repent, you have to make the most of his opportunity. Take him up on his offer, but don't take his offer for granted. You have no guarantee of another.

It's a bit like being in the wrong part of town after dark. You thought it would be fun, wild, and crazy. But now that the sun has gone down, it's more crazy and wild than you expected and not much fun. Storefronts are locked and barred. Shadowy figures in hooded sweatshirts, hands shoved deep in their pockets, slouch against buildings under broken streetlights. This is dangerous. You should not be here. You should not have come. You wanted the excitement, but now you're not sure you can afford the price.

Here's the spiritual paradox. If you desperately hope for a bus to come by to rescue you, God often sends one. But if you decide to let it pass, glibly assuming that there will always be another one, you are likely to find yourself vainly waiting in the dark. You'd be a fool to pass up the first bus and stay, wouldn't you? But think about your life: there's a world of difference between repeatedly failing and repeatedly refusing God's opportunities to deal with your failures. Aren't you foolish when you keep yelling at your kids instead of wrestling with God to learn his ways of parenting them? Aren't you a fool to favor another lusty look over actively embracing God's call to purity and fidelity? You know you're a fool when you'd rather harbor bitter grudges instead of longing for God to set you free to forgive. Whenever you pass up God's opportunities – whenever you don't use them fully – you're taking advantage of him. When you take his mercy lightly, you have no guarantee you'll get another chance.

Nina finally returned to God, but her delay cost her. The time she was almost run over was a bad moment. Even worse were the times she felt physically threatened or harassed by the company she kept. But most grievous and long lasting is her sadness over the time she wasted. She wishes she had those years back to grow in her knowledge and service of Christ. My greatest regret is also lost time. When I head for the fence instead of the shepherd, I ingrain patterns and attitudes that take additional time and energy to overcome. With each detour of reinforcing ungodliness that I must then unlearn, I forfeit some of my ability to serve in God's kingdom. In the moment, wasted time never feels like too much to pay, but later it always fuels regret. My sins are forgiven, but my regret is real.

In mercy, God gave Nina and Ahab many chances to repent, but they could not count on being offered any of them. Neither can you. God is merciful and he gives multiple chances, but he doesn't promise to keep on doing so. You don't know where or when, but there comes a point when God stops. It is in his gracious nature to offer, but don't presume upon his kindness. If he's giving you an opening now, take it. That way you can be sure it's not his last.

on your own

1 Where in your life has God offered you numerous second chances? Where has he given you multiple opportunities to repent? Thank him for his persevering kindness that led you to repent.

2 How long did it take you to respond to him? What kept you from taking advantage of his mercy earlier? Why did you resist for so long? Ask Jesus to forgive you for the desires that pushed him aside.

3 Is there currently an area in your life where you are resisting God? What lies are you telling yourself when he calls you to repent? What is it about your sin that you cherish enough to ignore your God as though he were an unwanted intruder?

4 Whether you're currently resisting the Lord or just remembering what that's like, ask him to renew you by his Spirit so that you will not take him and his mercy for granted. Ask for a repentant heart that hates evil and loves his ways.

How do you respond when Jesus intercedes for you?

Having more than one chance offers hope. But if all you have to rely on is your own resources, an extra chance is just one more opportunity to mess up.

Jason usually had a positive outlook on life. Even when life threw him a curve, he projected confidence that God still loved him and that everything was going to work out for the best. Not today. Something was troubling him. He didn't take long to confess, "I went out with some friends, had too many drinks, and sat up doing Ecstasy all night." What made his admission especially bitter was how quickly he had gone from feeling strong in his faith to reliving patterns he had hoped were behind him.

So Many Promises, So Few Kept

While the details may be alien to you, you probably can relate to Jason's experience. Think back to a particular sin that enslaved you for months or years. Then – miraculously! – by God's mercy you were set free. And you rejoiced! You vowed that from then on, life would be different. You began practicing disciplines intended to draw you closer to Christ and to his family; you experienced the joy of knowing him more deeply. You grew confident that this time really was different.

Then weeks, perhaps months later, you found yourself returning to the old patterns. You began wondering, *Have these last few weeks been a joke? Have I just been fooling myself? Am I really no different?* Discouragement joined those mocking self-assessments and brought self-loathing with it. Giving up seemed like a reasonable option. You went from valley to peak to valley: yet once you returned to the valley, what hope did you have? It seemed that even with Christ's initial involvement, your resolve was no match for what you were facing.

The discouraging cycle is easy to see with addictive substances because the contrast between peak and valley comes so quickly and dramatically. But all of us know what it feels like to commit ourselves to holiness, only to find ourselves doing the things we promised not to do. People vow not to punish their kids in anger and fail. They renounce gossip only to find themselves sharing juicy tidbits at the office coffee stand. You promised yourself – and your God – to be more patient with others while driving, not to lie to your boss, to only eat three-quarters of a cup of ice cream three times a week – and you have broken each promise. The children of Israel would have had great sympathy for you and me as they reflected on their experience at the base of Mount Sinai.

A Stiff-Necked People

Remember Mount Sinai? There, the newly liberated people met with God. He reminded them how he had rescued them and how he longed to make them his special people if they would keep his covenant. To this gracious offer, coming hard on the heels of their deliverance, the people responded, "We will do everything the Lord has said."[1] They prepared themselves to meet with God, heard him speak his commands, and celebrated the covenant God had initiated with a meal. The elders ate and drank in the presence of God! Then sadly, just a few weeks later, they broke their commitment, along with God's covenant, in spectacular fashion. They hosted another celebration meal – this one with their new god, thereby canceling out the earlier one blessed by their Deliverer.[2]

They sinned horribly. They had no idea how great their danger was. They spurned their one true lover, who had never forgotten them, and considered him faithless. When God witnessed their idolatrous adultery, he said to Moses (slightly paraphrased), "Step aside; I'm going to wipe them out!"

Do you have the picture? The people are partying down below without an inkling that they are about to be destroyed. Their eyes and ears function, but they don't see or hear rightly. They have heard God's words, but they don't connect them to their lives. They have everything they need for a godly life, but they don't respond in a way that will bring life. Instead, they revel in what will kill them. They are blind to reality.

Fortunately, Moses did recognize the danger the Israelites faced. He immediately placed himself between God and his people. Have you ever inserted yourself between an angry person and the object of his anger

---

[1] Ex. 19:8.
[2] Ex. 32:1-35.

and noticed that his anger shifts? Now he's mad at you. That's the danger Moses risked on Mount Sinai. God was justly angry with the Israelites; he had decided to destroy them, but Moses jumped in the middle! Clearly Moses was not acting in his own best interest.

Consider how unnatural his response was. Moses hadn't asked to lead God's people, and it had proven to be a task that was upsetting and inconvenient. They were not loveable people. They were uneducated, uncultured, and radically unwilling to change. Worse, while God demonstrated his commitment to them, keeping his promise made four hundred years earlier to free them, the Israelites remained committed only to themselves, reveling in their own pleasures and fears at the base of Sinai.

God characterized his wayward and stubborn people as "stiff-necked." Moses declared that they had "been rebellious against the LORD ever since I have known [them]."[3] Harsh? Yes, but accurate. In many ways, the Israelites showed contempt for God and for Moses as God's hand-picked deliverer. No sooner had God delivered them from Egypt than they accused him of intending to kill them at the Red Sea. Later, they sang the same refrain when they claimed that God was trying to starve them to death and when they feared dying of thirst. They were unpleasant, tiresome people. It would have been easy for Moses to justify turning his back on them. It would have been natural.

Moses, however, demonstrated something supernatural. He put his own comfort second to the need of God's people. He looked beyond their sin to the danger they were in. He cared about their plight when it would have been easier not to care. Interceding for them was not natural, but it was certainly necessary. Without it they were doomed. Having an intercessor who could deal "gently with those who [were] ignorant and [were] going astray" meant the difference between life and death for them.[4]

We are not told precisely why Moses had compassion for these obstinate people, but surely he was familiar with his own failings. Remember his early attempt at liberating the Israelites? It resulted in one dead Egyptian, the Israelites' rejection, and a flight for his life.[5] Remember when God told him to go speak to Pharaoh, but Moses suggested that God go find someone else?[6] Here was a man who was acquainted with faithlessness, both the presumptuous variety and the retreating kind. He knew something of human failings, but he also had experienced God's mercy and redeeming work in his own life.

---

[3] Deut. 9:13; Ex. 33:5; Deut. 9:24.
[4] Heb. 5:2.
[5] Ex. 2:11-15.
[6] Ex. 4:13.

Whatever the reason, Moses interceded for his people simply because of their need. He knew that their actions required someone to speak for them or they would be destroyed. They needed someone to step in and rescue them. And that is the crucial need of sinful, confused, and unhappy people in all times and places.

WANTED: INTERCESSORS

Moses' intercession worked, and God changed his mind! That raises lots of questions: Does God change his mind? *Can* he change his mind? The confusing fog that surrounds such questions allows something more crucial to be overlooked. God chooses to reveal his nature in the context of relationships. The text does not focus on the question of God changing his mind in an abstract way, as though it could be discussed apart from his relationship to his people. Instead, God relented after listening to Moses, who was the very person God had appointed to lead his people. In other words, God appointed the intercessor he was willing to hear.

This says things about God that are far more powerful and significant than an abstract debate about whether or not he changed his mind. If there had been no one to intercede, God would have destroyed the people; he was not playing a game with Moses. The people truly were in terrible danger. Yet God had already provided the solution to the problem Israel's sin had created. The passage, therefore, shows us God's heart for his people. He provided someone to intercede on their behalf. If you miss this, God looks like he doesn't know what's going to happen, like he isn't ruling his universe. He also looks unreasonable, like a cosmic bully on the verge of losing control. The passage does not downplay the explosive combination of a holy God with an evil people. Instead, it uses that reality to highlight the intercessor who was appointed by this same merciful God. Moses was able to stand effectively between God and the objects of his anger because of God's merciful initiative in placing him there.

This is not unique in God's dealings with humanity. Abraham had a similar role when he argued for the righteous who might be living in Sodom and Gomorrah.[7] Aaron later interceded for the people when God sent a plague, standing between the living and the dead so that the plague stopped.[8] God not only doesn't mind having people intercede, he goes out of his way to make sure they do. He is under no obligation to tell people his plans to punish or to discipline others; he needs neither their permission nor approval. Yet he seeks such encounters anyway.

---

[7] Gen. 18:22-33.
[8] Num. 16:48.

God appointed Moses to intercede, and the result is wonderful for the people. But in this case, it does not last. Indeed, it cannot. Eventually the people proved too much for Moses. He struck a rock angrily after God told him to speak mercifully.9 He disqualified himself from entering the Promised Land because he finally reached his limits with the people. He was not alone. Aaron failed so badly at that same moment that he did not enter the Promised Land either.10 As intercessors, they had their own shortcomings. They too needed someone to intercede for them.

Nothing captures God's combined desire and disappointment better than Ezekiel 22:30: "I looked for a man among them who would build up the wall and stand before me in the gap on behalf of the land so I would not have to destroy it, but I found none." God did not delight in destroying his people or the land. He longed for someone to build up his people and intercede for them. But he did not find the person who could satisfy that longing.

As we read through the Old Testament, we keep looking for the One who will be able to stand in the gap and intercede for us, without needing his own intercessor. God's people needed him. We need him. But we don't find him . . . until Jesus. In him, God supplies all we need. That means you are not alone when your actions betray your good resolutions. Jesus is praying for you.

DID YOU GET THAT? JESUS IS PRAYING FOR YOU

This is far more than a well-meaning counselor sending up a quick prayer. This is not a friend who asked for your help last week with his own sins. This is not someone on the outskirts of the power circles in heaven. This is Jesus, the Father's own Son. This is the Chosen One who functions now in his ordained role before the Father. Do you think his intercession will be fruitless? Do you think that somehow his prayers for you to turn from sin to holiness and fellowship with him will not be answered? That won't happen. It cannot! You will rise again from the ruin you make of your life and one day you will see Jesus. He intercedes for you so that you are not destroyed. You will be brought into the Promised Land.

If all you had going for you was your own feeble strength, you would be in trouble. But as a Christian, you have so much more! Even at your worst moment, your God throws himself into the fight to rescue you from your own evil inclinations. When you are fallen or struggling,

9 Num. 20:9-12.
10 Num. 20:1-13.

97

your Father has already appointed a resource outside yourself who propels you toward holiness and a relationship with him.

Remember Jason from the beginning of this chapter? Jason was learning things about the depth of his sinful desires. He saw that they did not lose their grip on his soul overnight. He was coming to understand the unrelenting nature of the spiritual battle, and he was learning how weak and frail he really was. But he was also learning that he had a friend – a high priest – in the battle. Not a "friend" who whipped him on from behind or held himself aloof while Jason floundered, but a friend whose inflexible devotion to his welfare gave Jason the courage not to give up even when he faced major setbacks. Jason was learning that failure – even the huge, neon-lights variety – would never have the last word on him because Jesus was constantly praying new words to intercede for him. With that intercession, Jason will always get up one time more than he gets knocked down.

on your own

1   Where do you need Jesus to intercede for you? What are you wrestling
    with that needs supernatural intervention to overcome?

2   Some people believe that God withholds himself from us until we get
    our act together. But he's not like that. Spend some time meditating on
    how he provided an intercessor for you before you sinned because he
    knew you would need one. How does that knowledge change your view
    of God? How does it affect your confidence in him?

3   Think carefully about what you should do, knowing that Jesus fights for
    you. How does his present intercession affect your life? Where does it
    give you courage to do what he's calling you to do? What will you do
    today that expresses your confidence in this God-appointed High Priest
    who is ministering on your behalf?

4   As Jesus works for you and in you, you become more like him. Therefore
    you want to do the things he's given his life to do. Think about someone in
    your life who needs an intercessor. Take a moment to pray for this person.

Do you embrace Jesus' restoration when you fall?

We have seen that our God gives you another chance to respond to him. He works on your behalf, giving you the help you need. But can you recover from your failures? Will he ever use you in his kingdom again, or have you been relegated to a dusty back shelf? People burdened by these questions – pastors who've been unfaithful, wives who have unbiblically divorced their husbands, friends who can't take back the hurtful things they've said – are amazed at what God teaches about himself through Aaron's life.

Aaron, Moses' brother, serves as his spokesman: God speaks to Moses, Moses speaks to Aaron, and Aaron speaks to Pharaoh. In the desert it becomes apparent that God destines Aaron for the priesthood. He is the one for whom the priestly clothes are designed, and the one God keeps talking about when discussing ordination ceremonies.[1] He has a bright future loaded with ministry possibilities.

Then, while Moses is on Mount Sinai talking with God, Aaron leads the people in idolatry and debauchery.[2] He yields to what the people want. Instead of functioning as high priest to lead them to God, he leads them into rebellion against him, and helps them break their commitment. Moses' words to him on the way down the mountain are pure rebuke. They offer no hope of restoration to the office that had been described. So what happens now? Will Aaron still be high priest or has he sinned so greatly that God will replace him with someone else? Can you hear the question in Aaron's mind and in the minds of the people?

---

[1] Ex. 28-29.
[2] Ex. 32.

AARON RECLAIMED

Against that background, God's installation of Aaron as high priest is awe-inspiring.[3] You learn once again that God's grace goes beyond Aaron's failure. Does that still surprise you? Are you used to thinking that God only helps those who help themselves? Or that he only uses those whose records are spotless? Look again. Aaron had every advantage and threw them all away. Yet even for Aaron, God accepts a sacrifice that atones for his great sin.

God's acceptance is demonstrated when his glory appears at the end of Aaron's ordination ceremony. Fire came out from his presence and consumed the burnt offering Aaron had prepared – instead of consuming Aaron or the Israelites.[4] God accepted the offering in place of the one who offered it. In response, God's people shouted for joy and fell face down. They now had a high priest who could mediate with God on their behalf. He was a high priest who could sympathize with their weaknesses because he knew what it was to fail in a big way. But he also knew what it was to experience a greater mercy that drew him back to God. It's a powerful story of redemption and reclamation.

But where do you find this ordination ceremony? It's in Leviticus. Leviticus?! When was the last time a friend helped you from the book of Leviticus? When was the last time you hurried to show a friend the glorious things God was teaching you in this book? When was the last time you even read it? Leviticus is not one of the books we readily turn to, but in it we meet a God firmly committed to restoring his people from the ruin they make of their lives.

LEVITICUS

This book was birthed amid radical unfaithfulness. Leviticus 26:46 tells us, "These are the decrees, the laws and the regulations that the LORD established on Mount Sinai between himself and the Israelites through Moses." We saw earlier that because Moses intervened, the people weren't destroyed after their sin, but the reality and consequences of their idolatry were still present. When you're carousing with calves, you're not thinking about the consequences of your actions. But what do you think the Israelites felt like when Moses came down from meeting with God and sobered them up? Here's the contrast: awesomely holy God and incredibly unholy people. How can there be any relationship?

---

[3] Lev. 8.
[4] Lev. 9:24.

They cannot even keep the covenant for two months! How can they hope to please him long term? It's great to have a perfect God want to live among you – if you're perfect.[5] But what if you're not?

Pastor Todd knew he was not. When he committed adultery, he was simultaneously unfaithful to his spouse and to his God. When Todd slept with another church staff member, he also betrayed his calling to watch over the flock God entrusted to him. There wasn't a relationship in his life that was unaffected by his sin, and he knew it. What he didn't know was how to handle any of it, especially his relationship with God.

Leviticus was written for Todd, for people who sin abysmally. And it was also written for people whose daily, mundane, faithless activities don't make headlines but just as surely estrange them from God and those around them. Because Leviticus was given to people who dismally failed to meet the standards of their holy God, you realize it is a manual on how to handle failure. In that sense, it is a hopeful book. It lays out all the ways people disrupt fellowship between themselves and God *and* what to do when that fellowship is broken. It helps you to understand that there is a faithful way to deal with your faithlessness. You can be faithful even after you've failed to be perfect. The first seven chapters of Leviticus explain what to do when you've sinned (intentionally or unintentionally) and then God presents Aaron's ordination account. Inserting this story among the laws reinforces the restorative nature of the book. Essentially God is saying, "If Aaron can sin as badly as he did and not only be for-given but installed as high priest, then there is hope for every single one of you. You can still be my people and I will wholeheartedly receive you."

Todd needed to hear that message. In the aftermath of his affair, he was bombarded by voices that said, "There is no hope for you!" Self-recriminations played endlessly during every waking hour. Being alienated and rejected by his former friends reinforced his "beyond salvage" status. Internal and external voices united, driving him to despair that no one could receive him. Yet God's dealings with Aaron contradicted such judgments and they spoke with a louder voice. Todd heard his God and ran to him. During those heart-rending times of guilt and self-recrimination, the Lord would break through his despair, reminding him that despite his failure, Todd was still his son. He reminded Todd that the quality (or lack) of his godliness didn't prove God loved him, but that Christ's sacrifice did. Todd slowly allowed truth to reshape his relationship with the Lord so that he could begin to deal with the horrible mess he had made.

---

[5] I cannot improve upon this phrase, which I owe to a presentation by Doug Green.

Leviticus reveals God's gracious character. At nearly the same moment that he calls his people into covenant with himself, he shows them how to deal with their inevitable failure to keep that covenant. Leviticus – and anywhere you see sacrifices – is all about how to live faithfully after being faithless. It's about how to restore fellowship with our God when we disobey him.

This is amazing when you consider what covenants are. Typically, the weaker partner of the covenant has the death penalty hanging over his head if he fails to keep his end of the bargain. But you see something different in Leviticus. You see provisions to deal with those failures that do not require the offender to die. They *do* require an awful lot of work as well as a substitute death, but that is a far better deal than the offender would have gotten anywhere else. Amazingly enough, in God's covenant making, the offended, not the offender, is the one who ultimately pays for the violation. Jesus dies in our place. He enters into relationship fully aware of the weaknesses of his people, and then provides an ongoing means of reconciliation with himself.

One underrated and underused picture of God's commitment to restored relationships comes when Moses returns to the camp during the golden calf carnival.[6] Moses has carried the tablets with the Ten Commandments down the mountain, but when he sees what is taking place, he throws them down, breaking them into pieces. Why? The popular answer is that he has lost his temper. The text does tell us he's angry, but it does not say that he smashed the tablets because he was raging out of control. The parallel passage in Deuteronomy 9:15-17 doesn't even mention anger. Instead, it emphasizes that in rejecting the Lord's commands by pursuing idolatry, the people have broken the covenant. When Moses realizes the covenant is shattered by their disobedience, he shatters the stones on which it was written. He does symbolically what the people have done in reality. Yet when God calls Moses to meet him again on the mountain, he tells him to bring new tablets. And then he rewrites the covenant.

Did you see it? The people break the covenant and God rewrites it. The people are the covenant breakers. God is the covenant keeper, whose keeping overcomes their breaking. The book of Leviticus makes it clear that God knows that the people will break the covenant even as he makes it

---

6 Ex. 32:1-20.

with them. He made it, they subsequently broke it, but the most enduring part of the story is that he provided ways for fellowship to be restored.

SIN IS NOT A LITTLE THING

The way back to God is not easy, however. Read Leviticus carefully if you are tempted to think that "little" sins are no big deal. As you read page after page of how to deal with sin and what to do to restore a relationship with God, you will start to realize that sin is a very big deal. It creates barriers to communing with God that take huge amounts of time, energy, and material to remove. Sin creates, in the strict sense of the words, a bloody mess. Yet I often hear people minimize how deeply sin affronts God and harms other people.

In *The Bourne Supremacy*, Jason Bourne, played by Matt Damon, wrestles with flashbacks of his earlier, forgotten life as an assassin. Although he has renounced his past, he is haunted by a memory of murdering Irena Neski's parents. Those deaths were made to look like a murder-suicide committed by Irena's mother. Perhaps a decade later, driven by remorse, he searches Irena out at great personal risk to confess what he's done. He hopes that the knowledge will bring healing to her feelings toward her parents. The scene nearly strikes you as Christian until he abruptly mumbles, "I'm sorry," and trudges out the door.

Jason Bourne is responsible for impoverishing Irena's life in more ways than he can ever understand. He can't know the pain that wracked her mind and body. He hasn't experienced the burden she has lived with for years, believing her mother murdered her father, wondering why. He doesn't know what dangers or taunts he exposed her to by depriving her of her closest guardians. He ripped the center out of her world and then has the gall to brusquely re-enter it – uninvited – peeling open old wounds with no salve to offer. The best he can do is manage a feeble, "I'm sorry." It's monstrous! Bourne shows he has no appreciation for the way he's affected Irena.

Yet his crime is my crime and yours. We do and say things that leave people devastated: we deceive our parents, verbally attack our friends, harbor bitter grudges, are unfaithful – and then say, "I'm sorry." Sure, we're sincere, but we're utterly ignorant of the effect we've had. Then, to add insult to injury, we get offended when the other person doesn't quickly forgive and forget. We have so little idea what we do to each other.

We have even less of an understanding of how sin affects God. Have you ever realized you've sinned against a holy God and found yourself wondering, *What can I do to fix this and make things right?* There are steps toward God that are appropriate, but you're as deceived as the unmerciful servant if you think you can make things right.[7] Remember the servant who owed his master 10,000 talents? If you convert that into today's income levels, that's somewhere between seven and twelve *billion* dollars of debt![8] He says to his master, "Be patient with me and I will pay it all." Be patient? Are you kidding? How will you ever amass that amount of money to pay the master back? The servant is fooling himself into thinking it's not really much of a debt at all. Yet even if he could pay it back, how would he remove the impact of his irresponsibility from his master's mind?

Leviticus sobers you with all its arduous means of dealing with sin. It requires you to realize that sin is not a little thing, easily remedied with minimal effort. Instead, it clearly points to Christ's sacrifice, where sin cost Jesus his life. When you think about Jesus having to die, it makes all your attempts at penance seem ridiculous and offensive. If there had been any other way to deal with sin, God would not have sent Jesus, and Jesus would not have had to die. When I face the awful reality of the cross, I see that my attempts to live the Christian life, apart from daily dependence on Christ, make a mockery of what he has done. In Jesus Christ, one sacrifice took place once for all.[9] The tortuous means of reconciling a relationship between a holy God and a covenant breaker has been taken out of my hands and completed by God himself.

This is not to say that Aaron and Todd had nothing to do after their sins. Reconciliation is the starting point for the ongoing battle of faith. Despair's tentacles lurk around every corner, tempting you to believe that not even Jesus can bring glory out of the mess you made. How about the struggle to believe that his sacrifice, atonement, and forgiveness have greater weight than your sin? How do you overcome the despondency brought on by those side-long glances from people who look down on you? Overcoming the personal debilitating effects of sin requires consistent effort. Engaging in the battle can be exhausting, and we've not even considered the interpersonal dimension. Without the certainty of God's commitment to keep the covenant intact, we would quickly be overwhelmed, lose heart, and quit.

---

[7] Matt. 18:21-35.

[8] Assuming a talent is equivalent to twenty years wages and an annual average wage is somewhere between $35,000-$50,000.

[9] Heb. 9:26.

INVITATION TO RELATIONSHIP

You need to realize, however, that Leviticus is not simply a reference manual that tells you what to do and how to do it. It is given by God for a purpose – to restore relationship between you and him. The requirements of Leviticus, like all the Law, have been fully met for us in Christ, but there is still great value in reading the book because it shows you God's heart. The content of the book and the fact that the Lord wanted it included in the Bible reflect his desire to restore. The book reflects his *desire* for you to live on good terms with him as he lives with you, to be friends with you. That means you need to read it as an invitation from him to be restored.

In our office buildings, the guidelines for fire alarms lay out what you are to do and how you are to do it: "Turn right and walk three doors to the stairwell. Walk down the stairs to the ground floor. Do NOT use the elevator during an emergency." But the people who wrote those instructions weren't longing for you to use them. They would be much happier if the need never arose.

God in Leviticus is different. He longed for the guidelines to be used because the need already existed, and following the guidelines would result in full restoration with himself. You cannot read this book without recognizing his invitation, and you cannot recognize the invitation without responding to him.

If there is a fire in your office building, you have to make a faith-based choice. If you believe that the person who wrote the guidelines was competent and dedicated to your best interests, you will follow his instructions to the letter. If not, you will trust yourself to find your own way out. The same is true of Leviticus. If you believe God's invitation of friendship, you will do what he says. You'll come quickly to him when you fail, confident that he will receive you. If, however, you believe that he would never befriend such a disappointment as yourself, and that you'll never be good enough, you won't obey him. You won't come. And if you didn't believe that someone so powerful was willing to receive you, your refusal would make sense.

In other words, the true foundation of Leviticus, the penultimate "Book of the Law," is faith. You would only do the things Leviticus prescribes – offer sacrifices for sins, carry out purification ceremonies, and make endless clean-unclean decisions – if you trusted that God is who he says he is and does what he says he does. Before Aaron could serve as high priest, he had to believe that, according to God's word, he had been purified. Before Todd could begin thinking about how to love his family after the devastation he had caused, he had to believe that Christ's sacrifice made him holy and acceptable to God. Before you can confidently rely on Christ's power in you, you have to believe that he has already gladly created a way for you to deal with your worst sins and failures.

on your own

1   You, like every Christian, have made promises to God – and then broken them. Do you wonder how any future promises to love and serve him will have any integrity or credibility? How do God's provisions for covenant breakers of the past help you see how to handle your own broken promises?

2   You might be someone who has sinned so badly that you don't believe that God could ever use you again to help someone else. How do God's actions in Aaron's story encourage you to hope?

3   Do you find yourself in a paradoxical place where you feel as if God could never forgive you, yet you treat lightly the ways you sin against others? ("It wasn't that big a deal." "She'll get over it." "What I did wasn't as bad as what he did to me.") Take some time to consider how seriously God takes sin. Do you believe your debt is calculated in the billions? Did it really cost a life of infinite value to pay what you owed? Ask Jesus to soften your conscience so that you learn to hate the things he hates with the same intensity.

4   Think of someone who needs to hear how God's mercy and forgiveness go deeper than anything he or she has done. How will you start to share this with him or her? Write down one person's name and begin praying for an opportunity to share this gift with him or her.

Do you realize Jesus never leaves you on your own?

Despite God's encouragement and resources, sometimes we're too scared even to try to obey him. We get spiritual stage fright. Everyone has had some experience with stage fright, that pressured combination of trying to succeed by your own efforts and the confident knowledge that you will fail. You prepare for an event and then, when it arrives, you can't perform at your peak. And so your fear ensures that you won't do your best.

I remember a cold, rainy Saturday when I was in high school. There was a track meet scheduled and I was nervous. Most track events are very individualistic and highly visible. There is no way to hide a sub-par performance because everyone sees what you've done. My gloomy thoughts matched the day's damp grayness. Earlier that month we had had a meet postponed because of the weather and I was hoping – praying – that this one would be also. It wasn't.

Standing there in the cold morning drizzle, I was miserable. I considered all the things that could – would – go wrong: how long the race was, how much it hurt to sprint that far, and how much faster the other guys probably were. Mentally, I was unprepared for the starting gun and, not surprisingly, I performed poorly. I had talked myself out of the race before it began.

I am reminded of this experience when God leads me to a place where I don't feel strong, ready, or prepared. Remaining patient and compassionate while helping a resistant child with homework seems impossible. Talking as candidly about God with unbelieving friends as I do with believing ones remains a challenge. Let's not even discuss seeing baked goods at the office while I'm counting calories. Some activities seem doomed from the start. My resources are so dwarfed by the requirements of the task that failure seems inevitable. And so I talk myself out of even trying to pursue godliness in the middle of my circumstances. I easily give in to impatience, hypocrisy . . . and doughnuts.

This defeated attitude is present in all our lives: Husbands who have given up discussing certain topics with their wives because they "know" what their wives will say. Mothers who no longer try to train their children because nothing seems to work. Men who feel that the allure of pornography will always win. Women who feel hopelessly driven to attain a perfect body. When these people face the tough battles, they dwell on the reasons why they'll be defeated. Daily life calls for consistent heroic efforts for which our resources seem wholly inadequate.

The children of Israel could definitely relate.

FEARFUL OF GOD'S CALL

On the eve of entering the Promised Land, Moses stood on the edge of the desert and preached a sermon series that became the book of Deuteronomy. The children of Israel desperately needed to hear what he had to say. Sure, the desert years were behind them, but the conquest of Canaan lay ahead. They still had to deal with the "giants" who lived in the land, and those indigenous peoples had not grown shorter or less numerous, nor had their cities decayed, during the years the Israelites had wandered in the wilderness. Taking the land from them was still a frightening prospect.

An earlier generation stood at this exact spot forty years earlier and balked. God told them to take the land and they told God to take a hike. Can you hear their children asking, "What hope do we have? Our parents, who saw all the powerful things God did to the Egyptians, blew it when they got here. If they couldn't trust God, what chance do we have?"

They were not a trained army outfitted with the latest battle gear. They were former slaves, refugees fleeing genocide, desert nomads. No matter how you look at it, they were anything but competent warriors. Sure, they had just won a couple of battles, but nothing like what they were about to face.

Worst of all, Moses was staying behind. He was the one who had faced down Pharaoh; he hadn't panicked with everyone else at the Red Sea. More importantly, he was the one who had shepherded and led them all those years and interceded for them with God. He was their God connection. How could they consider entering the land without him?

You can hear the unasked question permeating the assembly as it gathered before Moses: "Do we dare even try what God has called us to do?"

Over and over in Deuteronomy, God tells them not to be afraid and speaks words of comfort to them. That's encouraging. But does he provide anything else for his fearful people as he gives them an impossible assignment?

Let me suggest that you read through Deuteronomy using an inexpensive Bible or computer printout. Underline or highlight every time God talks about himself in relation to his people. You will be amazed at how often he does so. Repeatedly, he reminds the Israelites that he has fought for them, carried them through the desert, and provided for all their needs. He reviews the promises he's made in the past to reinforce the fact that he fully intends to keep them. He gives them new promises too: that he will not leave them or destroy them; that he will not forget his covenant with them; that he will bless them, give them a land flowing with milk and honey, and enlarge their territory.

I am amazed at how often God reminds his people of what he has done for them and what he will do. Apparently he thinks this is pretty important, considering that the Israelites who heard these sermons were being reminded of events that had happened in their lifetimes. They had either heard these stories about God's mercy from their parents or tasted his daily grace in the wilderness firsthand. Yet God still believed he needed to remind them. If that is so, we certainly need to be reminded of these examples from centuries ago.

As you highlight what God says about himself, pay attention to how closely he links his reminders with his commands. You start to see a structure emerge: (1) Here is what I have done for you, (2) Now you are able to please me, (3) Therefore, obey my commands. God often reminds his people of what he has done for them while instructing them on how to respond. He works tirelessly to tie faith and obedience together. This is true for you as well. He does not expect you to make the first move so that he will reward you. Instead, he has moved toward you first, giving you faith, so that you can respond in the way he requires. He expects you to respond, but he has done the work that makes your response possible.

By linking his past actions for you with his present commands to you, he doesn't let you think that you can obey apart from believing what he has said. Obedience cannot be separated from belief. If Israel is going to take the land, it is because they believe his promise to give it to them. If they don't go, it is because they do not believe him. Their actions and ours – our obedience or disobedience – express our faith.

This sounds a lot like the apostle Paul's way of reasoning: because Jesus has set you free from sin and death, you are now free to serve him.[1] You respond in accordance with your conviction that you really are free. Obedience is not optional for the Christian, but it is always a response to God based on what he has already done. That's why God reminds us so often.

GOD GIVES EVEN MORE THAN ACTIONS

God offers his fearful people reminders of what he has already done for them, but most importantly he offers himself. Over and over in Deuteronomy, he promises to be with them. That's a nice offer, but sometimes it can seem disconnected from my struggles. When it comes to the faith-stretching things that require real practical help and resources – living with a special needs child, caring for a parent with Alzheimer's, confronting a manipulative coworker, or reining in my abusive tongue – God's offer to be with me doesn't seem to meet the need.

In Exodus 3:9-12, God appoints Moses to deliver the Israelites from Pharaoh's tyranny. God calls Moses to go and Moses reminds God of his inadequacies: "Who am I, that I should go to Pharaoh and bring the Israelites out of Egypt?" To which God responds, "I will be with you" and gives him a sign to encourage him. Is that a satisfying answer to you? Moses didn't think so as he proposed that God find someone else. To some degree I find myself in Moses' camp. If God wants me to take on Pharaoh, I want a rocket launcher! I want something I can feel, touch, hold, and control. But God doesn't give me those things. He gives me his promise to be with me. What good is that?! And that's when it hits me. When I allow my thoughts to become words, I am stunned at the depth of my unbelief. What more could God offer me? There is nothing greater in the universe to give me! Yet somehow, I don't believe it's enough.

When we lived in Philadelphia, my wife came home from work very upset one evening. As she was walking down the street, some young boys had been throwing rocks at her (my in-laws are going to be thrilled to hear this story!). I jumped up and asked a friend to go with me to confront the kids. We found one of them, who immediately got very scared. He denied having any part in the rock-throwing and was very willing to implicate others down the street. Playing along as though I believed he had nothing to do with it, I asked him to relay our concerns

---

1 See 2 Cor. 5:15; Rom. 6:15-18; Gal. 5:1; Eph. 2:1-10; Col. 3:1-17.

to the other boys, which he eagerly promised to do. That was the end of the rock-throwing incidents.

Why did my words have such an impact? I'm not very big. I didn't scowl, threaten, wave a gun, or call the police. In fact, under the circumstances, I was remarkably restrained, calm, and polite. The reason my words had such an impact was because Bryan was with me. He stood behind me – six-foot-four, 260 pounds, wearing a black leather jacket, dark sunglasses, and a frown. A former Navy Seal with a black belt in some martial art I've since forgotten, Bryan could intimidate just by standing still. The impact I had – and my lack of fear in confronting those kids – came from the person I was with.

Jesus makes Bryan look puny. Yet I don't believe he's enough because I want something more tangible. I don't really believe that having the Creator and Sustainer of the universe with me is worth very much. My response demonstrates that I think he is inadequate to help with real trouble. Once again, it's time to repent of unbelief.

If we look ahead to see how the promises of Deuteronomy are more deeply and completely fulfilled in Christ, God's promise becomes infinitely more powerful. The Israelites feared losing Moses, but we never lose our Deliverer. He lives today interceding for us. He has poured out his Holy Spirit into us so that we are never separated from him. We have Immanuel – God with us. We walk through life with One who promises he will never leave us or forsake us; we can connect with him at any moment. Do your reactions to life's challenges show that you believe he is all you will ever need, or do they reveal that you long for something more?

CONDITIONAL UNCONDITIONALITY

You might be thinking, *But there are many times when I have believed Jesus was with me and things still did not work out. I did what I was supposed to do and other people did not reciprocate. My friends, spouse, or children did not respond well. The doughnuts won again. Anger and impatience crushed kindness and patience. Everything went badly – just like I knew it would.*

In other words, when you tried to live on the basis of what you believed was true, you walked away more despondent than ever. When you discussed this with other Christians, they suggested that maybe you hadn't been faithful enough. They said that if you expected to receive anything from God, you had to ask without doubting. But you didn't know how to be more faithful, so you quit hoping, talking yourself out of the game before it began.

As you look at God's call to his children to enter the Land, or to Moses to free his people, you realize that his instructions were not arbitrary. God did not order those things as extreme tests to develop his people's faith. Those specific events were necessary to bring about his greater purposes of redemption. His people had to be freed from the bondage of slavery (Egypt) so that they could obey him. They had to actively fight against influences (Canaanites) that would tempt them, lead them astray, and re-enslave them. Anything short of these goals would distract his people from serving and enjoying him, ultimately ending up in their rejecting him. His commands furthered his plan to establish a holy people for himself that would bless the whole earth. When he promised to go with them, he gave them an ironclad guarantee that his plans would not fail.

Yet his promised presence came with the expectation that his people were moving in his direction. Often when I think God has failed me – that his presence wasn't enough – I find upon reflection that I've tried to force him to go along with my agenda. Or I've wanted his help for the wrong reasons. James discusses this situation when he says that we sometimes don't get what we ask God for because we're set on using it for our own purposes in life.[2] And God doesn't play along.

Since the cross and resurrection, we recognize that the greatest enemies to godliness are not outside us but within. We want what we want more than we want what God wants. We want nice interactions with people more than we want to respond the way Jesus would to difficult situations. We want comfortable lives more than we want to depend on Christ for his daily provisions. We want something besides what God wants or promises, yet we get upset when we think we've exercised faith and our hopes remain unrealized. We are very willing to live "Christianly" if it makes our lives better. But when Christian living makes life harder, we lose our zeal for following Jesus. Obeying God's call did not make the Israelites' lives nicer. They escaped Egypt to walk in the harsh desert. They evicted the Canaanites only to face ungodliness among their own tribes.

If you are controlled by an agenda other than growth in godliness and a Christ-like love for others, you will be overwhelmed by your inabilities and the situation's impossibilities. You will decide in advance to cut yourself out of the action because you don't expect to make a difference anyway. With that perspective, God's promise to be with you can seem weak. But

---

2 James 4:3.

if you want his will to be done and realize that he will not fail to bring it about in your life, his presence is more than comforting. It's more than a consolation prize substituting for what you really wanted – a girlfriend, a BMW, helpful children. His presence is real. It is energizing; it will give you courage to engage the impossible task he has given you to bring about his purposes in setting you free.

Begin by focusing on the differences God intends to make in you. I recall hearing a story about a nuclear protester. Apparently he was protesting all alone outside a power station. There was no crowd in attendance, no newsmen recording sound bites or capturing iconic images. Just one lonely man with a sign, pacing along a fence in the middle of nowhere. A person stopped by and asked a question intended to wake the man up to the real world: "Do you expect that by doing this you will change the world?" The protester responded, "No. I expect that doing this will change me."

Does that seem like a goal worth having? Is it worth the sacrifice of some of your comfort and agendas? If you insist on your own agenda, the protester's response will seem hopelessly discouraging. But if you want to line up with God's plans, his response will captivate you. God's presence with you will become inordinately generous.

on your own

1   What has God called you to do that absolutely petrifies you? Where is
    his call leading that you don't want to go?

2   How have your fears dwarfed his promise to be with you? Where do you
    struggle to believe that he is really all you need? Spend some time confessing
    your fear and your unbelief that he'll make a difference.

3   Fear often comes from feeling all alone as we do something difficult.
    Yet, thanks to Jesus, we're never alone. Try picturing Jesus at your side
    as you go. How would his presence there affect your attitude? How
    would you think differently? What would you do differently? In other
    words, if you truly believed Jesus was with you as he has promised, how
    would life be different for you?

4   Reflect back to other times in your life when you were scared, yet you
    obeyed your Lord's directions. Remind yourself how he met your needs.
    Spend some time praising him for how he came through in the past. Ask
    him to build your confidence that he will come through for you again.

Do you long for Jesus' transforming presence?

Ebenezer Scrooge – a stingy, small-souled man who cared more for wealth than for his fellow human beings. We readily apply his name to present-day misers. An awful, hateful man. How many misers do you both know and love? There's something about tight-fisted people that repulses us. God intended us to be benevolent stewards over his creation, but misers overturn this calling by slavishly serving money. These fallen images of God trade away his glory, exposing the dehumanizing results of idolatry. Scrooge, the consummate miser, would be better forgotten, useful only as a negative example to scare our children away from greed. But he's not forgotten. Quite the opposite: he's popular.

THE EBENEZER OBSESSION

Dickens's classic continues to be loved, cherished, and endlessly retold. I cannot begin to count the productions I've seen, ranging from the comic to the serious. What gives such life to a tale about one evil, pathetic, foolish man? I suspect that in part it reflects our own longing for the second chance Scrooge gets. We see in ourselves hints of his indifference to human need, egged on by our obsession with our own well-being, and we too wish for a chance to be free.

And yet, in the U.S., second chances are expected and largely unremarkable. They are part of our American optimism that life can always be better. As such, they are often taken for granted. Maybe, then, it's not so much the chance Scrooge is offered as what he does with it. Scrooge, like Bill Murray's character in *Groundhog Day*, takes advantage of his opportunity and becomes a dramatically different person. We are not simply captivated by a striking illustration of evil or the promise of a second chance. We are captivated by a person whose life changed 180 degrees for the better; a person like Zacchaeus.

THIEF TO PHILANTHROPIST OVER DINNER

God has always wanted his people to care about the poor and disenfranchised. Never were they to take advantage of others worse off than themselves. His concern undergirds one of the prophets' recurring indictments: that God's people failed to care for the poor among them and, even worse, stole from the poor to enrich themselves.

While eating dinner with Jesus, we've seen that Zacchaeus spontaneously announced that he would give half of all he owned to the poor.[1] Beyond that, he would return four times the amount he had stolen from others. Zacchaeus did a complete about-face in two areas that had vividly displayed his opposition to God. In so doing, he was admitting that he had committed the very sins that had led to Israel's exile. He openly acknowledged areas of his life that were offensive to God, areas he had previously disregarded. What is more, his efforts to reverse the evil he had done would likely cost him plenty and perhaps even ruin him financially. Zacchaeus' statement is not just polite, dinnertime small talk.

As Enron's stock price began falling in the autumn of 2000, its leaders repeatedly promised investors that it would rise again after a brief dip. Nevertheless, executives who understood the deeper problems within the company quietly sold their shares, driving the price even lower. Meanwhile, the company's rank and file, whose pension funds were dangerously overcommitted to company stock, were prevented by company regulations from selling. They watched helplessly over the next year as their accounts evaporated, leaving them with little for their future. Now imagine hearing that Enron's top executives were suddenly and voluntarily restoring those pensions out of their own wealth. You would know that something big had happened to change them deeply on the inside. Such a turnaround would be on par with what happened to Zacchaeus. Something major had just happened to turn a greedy, avaricious man into a giving person.

His life orientation was no longer directed inward toward himself but outward toward others. Like Scrooge, Zacchaeus's instincts were altered so that he saw people as individuals to serve rather than objects to exploit. He recognized he'd intentionally harmed other people and wanted to make things right. He could not undo the past, but he could give back (with excessive interest) what he had taken. Zacchaeus was a very different man. You see the new man in the actions that would have

---

[1] Luke 19:1-10.

once been alien to him. The lost man has been found because he responded to Jesus in a whole new way.

But when you study the passage to discover what produced such an amazing response, the text is curiously quiet. You know absolutely nothing about the conversation (if there was one) between Jesus and Zacchaeus during dinner. Luke records no sermon on sin, grace, and God's free gift. You're not told that Zacchaeus prayed a "sinner's prayer" ending with "in Jesus' name, amen." Not one key "witnessing tool" of the last century is in evidence, yet Zacchaeus suddenly confesses ways in which he had wronged people.

Zacchaeus was a new man, and what made him new was his encounter with Jesus. The critical factor in Zacchaeus's renewal was not what he learned or had been taught, but whom he'd been with. You are forced to look past whatever he and Jesus said to focus on the simple fact that Zacchaeus encountered Jesus.

In the presence of God, Zacchaeus experienced personal, specific conviction. Yet it was not conviction that produced despair – he was, after all, with the person who sought him out despite knowing who and what he was. In his case, conviction produced salvation that changed his life. Because his heart was touched by God, caring for the people God cares for became far more precious to him than the wealth he had amassed over the years.

It's not enough to analyze your life, to reflect on what you've done wrong, or to meditate on how great God is. All those things are worthwhile, but they never substitute for actually meeting Jesus. They can pave the way to such an encounter by helping you see your need for Christ. But renewal and change grow out of being with Jesus. To put it more strongly: being with Jesus irresistibly changes you.

CALVIN VS. DANIEL

Currently, "change" is a bit out of fashion. We are more likely to be encouraged to "be who you are" or "be authentic." Suggesting that a person do things differently feels like simple external image management divorced from the "real you." Somehow, to be different from what you have been is seen as putting on an act. From that perspective, change implies that you're an imposter.

We all know people for whom that idea is true: people who say the right words without meaning them. People who try on various personas like off-the-rack suits – street tough, self-absorbed diva, conservation-conscious granola. Such personas ring false because they are added from the outside rather than nurtured from within. We call such people phonies, poseurs, or hypocrites. We rightly want nothing to do with their kind of change.

But gospel change is different. It is not a high-powered Madison Avenue marketing veneer overlaid onto a deformed character. Gospel change has substance because it takes place internally. It radically reorients you to life so that you long for things that are the opposite of what you once desired. You are truly different because you are motivated to move toward God and those around you, instead of being self-absorbed. People who encounter Christ are not simply trying to marry new actions to a pre-existing selfish frame of reference. They experience a fundamental change that remakes them from the inside out. They act in accordance with a new gyroscope. Seeing the outward evidence of this inward reorientation, Jesus declared that salvation had in fact taken place in Zacchaeus's life.[2]

Do you remember Bill Watterson's *Calvin and Hobbes*? One frequent theme in that comic strip was how gifted Calvin was at avoiding baths. He complained, grumbled, and hid from his mom, making bath time a real struggle. One classic strip shows his mother searching for him through the house, to no avail. Finally, you see Calvin sitting on the roof, smiling impishly, and wondering when his mother will see that trying to get him into the tub just isn't worth the trouble.

Contrast that picture with my son Danny who, when he was about a year and a half, my father dubbed "Mr. Clean." Danny never liked dirty hands. He learned to eat with utensils early to avoid picking up food with his fingers. He didn't like messy dinners and always sat patiently to get washed up. (I know; I wouldn't have believed it either if I hadn't been there!) This mealtime enjoyment of cleanliness, however, paled in comparison to bath time. I wish you could have seen the excitement in our house! He absolutely loved being in water. I loved seeing his short, chubby legs pounding as he raced into the bathroom. He literally shook with excitement as he watched the tub filling, cheering the water on from the sidelines. I don't think it ever filled fast enough! Danny never had to be coerced to get washed, and he still doesn't. He longs for it. It

---

[2] Luke 19:9.

is something intrinsic to who he is. He values being clean and will do whatever it takes to accomplish that result.

Not so for Calvin. For Calvin to proclaim that he enjoyed taking a bath would be completely false; it runs counter to his nature. For Calvin, simply cooperating in getting washed would require a miracle. And yet that miracle is exactly what happens when God seeks and finds you. He doesn't make Calvins act opposite to their orientation so that they reluctantly go through the motions of taking a bath, loathing it the whole time. Instead he seeks out us Calvins, meets us where we are, and transforms us into Dannys. Because we really are different people after we meet him, we desire different things than we once did.

WALLFLOWER TO STREET PREACHER

I have been wonderfully surprised by this dynamic in my own life. For as long as I can remember, I've been scared of what other people thought of me. I've wasted enormous energy thinking about what to do or say in various situations so as not to give offense or stand out. Evangelistic outreaches used to kill me. That is one place where you just cannot hide, which makes it the worst activity for a people pleaser.

I had a friend at college who absolutely did not care what other people thought of him. Once he insisted that I help him hand out gospel tracts in the school's courtyard. I dutifully followed along while dying the thousand deaths of a coward. Afterward I made it very clear that I was simply never going to do that again. Unfortunately, this friend ended up walking away from the faith and we lost touch until a few years later. We met in the same courtyard, right after the college fellowship group had performed some street theater that concluded with me preaching! He and I sat down to talk and, predictably, he dismissed most of what I said about the Lord as theoretical and unrealistic. But then I reminded him of what I'd been like several years earlier. I asked him how he could account for the difference in me if the Lord were not real. That was perhaps the first time I had seen him speechless. He had answers for everything theological, but he could neither explain nor deny the dramatic and concrete change in me.

This has been true throughout my life. The same grace that moves me away from fearing people has also made me into a more patient, kind, and thoughtful person. Yes, change has been slow and is far from complete (I actually felt nauseated before speaking in the school's courtyard and you can ask my family about the progress I have yet to make with patience!) but it comes from sincere desires the Lord has put within me. Being with Jesus changes you. It's more dramatic for some than others, but it is true for all of God's children. Do you believe that Jesus can change you? Perhaps you genuinely believe that he cares for you and wants to come near to you but that he's powerless against what enslaves you.

I know a young man who sadly decided just that. He believed that sin would always master him and that it was useless to fight it. Yes, Jesus loved him, but God wasn't going to change him. This friend decided that the best he could do was try to limit sin by indulging himself in small ways he hoped wouldn't ruin his life. He assumed that he would never see substantial change in his life, so he just tried to keep sin from running out of control. Unfortunately for him, that's not the way life works. You cannot contain or manage sin. You either grow in holiness or you perfect evil. He made an awful decision that, in his frustration, made sense to him.

Does his way of dealing with sin make sense to you? Do you try to minimize the fallout instead of fighting because you think it won't make any difference? Has pornography, a critical spirit, impatience, or gluttony so overpowered you that you've lost your willingness to fight? Have you conceded the battle before it's begun? Here again, it starts as a matter of faith: "Jesus, help me to believe that simply being with you changes people so radically that they no longer seek the things they once did. Help me to believe that I will not always be bound in and by sin. Let me believe that, as with Zacchaeus, you can renew my heart so that I long for good things. Give me courage to fight the battle just one more day."

Can it really be that simple? Or are you too jaded by experience to hear what I've just said? What I said in the earlier chapters is true: being a faithful Christian is different from being a perfect person. There is no evidence that Zacchaeus became perfect, but certainly he was changed dramatically. God moves toward people with a purpose. He seeks you out to change you at your core, so that you move in the opposite direction from what motivated you before you met him. It's not complicated. As your relationship with Jesus grows, you become dissatisfied with a self-absorbed way of life. You long instead to live differently. Such a longing can't help but express itself.

on your own

1   What negatively defines you? Compulsive lying, fearing other people, a sarcastic edge? Other people can often offer insight into problems you don't see, so ask your friends what they think you most need to work on.

2   Next, consider how that sinful pattern hurts the people around you. Ask yourself: In what ways does this pattern drag others down? How do I make it hard on other people to live or work with me? Instead of building others up, how do I tear them down? Ask people around you, "How does my _____ affect you?"

3   Thinking about these things is important but, as you know, thinking is not the same as changing. You need to meet with Jesus. Ask him to help you hate what you do to others. Ask him to give you his heart for others so that you love them as he loves you.

4   Now put some thought into what a 180° change would look like. What would help the people you've hurt? What do you need to start doing? Go to the people closest to you and put your faith into practice by loving them in ways that counter how you've hurt them.

Part IV

God radically transforms you

Everyone who has been pursued by God has been transformed. He came to them in their need and gave them exactly what they needed. Dramatic change occurred because a very great God stepped into their very little world. However, we often don't know what to anticipate in terms of the changes he will make. Consequently, we wind up looking for evidence of his work in the wrong places.

Contrary to our desire for God to change other people to make us more comfortable, he often changes us so that we will bring his comfort – and his call – to others. He works to change the people around you by introducing himself to them through you. He doesn't work to make you comfortable. He works to make you holy so that you can help other people experience his holiness. When people experience holiness, they learn to long for something bigger, different, and more wonderful than what they've got. This final section shows you the kinds of changes you can expect from a loving God as he transforms your heart, mind, and soul.

Are you growing in humble honesty? 16

The second presidential debate of the 2004 election closed with an extremely difficult question. Linda Grabel asked, "President Bush, during the last four years, you have made thousands of decisions that have affected millions of lives. Please give three instances in which you came to realize you had made a wrong decision and what you did to correct it."

What a great question! You want leaders whose humility allows them to thoughtfully acknowledge where they didn't do their best. Yet, simultaneously, what an awful question! Who likes admitting mistakes or errors? Can you imagine being asked at next year's performance review to name three ways you hurt the company? How about if your spouse or best friend – or better yet, your child – asked you to list three times you've mistreated him or her?

INVITATION TO HUMILITY

I wonder what it was like for President Bush to try to answer that question on live TV. I had a hard enough time in my living room. I thought about it for 8.5 seconds and then distracted myself by thinking about something else. Try asking yourself now . . . done already? Ironic, isn't it? We long for humility in others yet shy away from developing too much of our own. Linda Grabel asked a hard question.

What makes this question difficult is the willingness it requires to assess who you are and what you've done. Self-examination is difficult because we don't like the results. In other words, most of us don't ask how we're doing because we don't want to know. We don't want to face ourselves, so we don't look. It might upset our cherished notions that we are reasonably decent human beings. But people who are touched by God are willing to start looking because they have experienced God's love.

Not the Man He Thought He Was

If you look at yourself from a human vantage point, you can often be convinced that you're doing as well as can be expected. You're not perfect, but you provide for your family's needs, take care of your possessions responsibly, willingly talk about Christ at work, and even volunteer for nursery duty at church! But when you begin to view your life from God's perspective, those conclusions are sometimes exposed as ignorant and foolish. Seemingly solid advantages crumble, revealing motives that on second glance are actually self-serving. At times you busy yourself providing for others to avoid getting close to people; you like taking care of your possessions in order to be envied; talking about Christ at work keeps people from learning about your problems at home; and you often serve the church out of guilt, not thankfulness. Under God's gaze, the brilliant façade of your life too often disappears to reveal a rotten frame underneath.

The prophet Isaiah discovered the rottenness in his life when he saw himself from God's perspective. On the surface he looked pretty good. He was a religious man who married well (to a prophetess) and had at least two sons. He was connected politically through his cousin, King Uzziah, and was an advisor to kings. This position gave him acceptance and access to the inner circles of power that few of Israel's prophets ever enjoyed.

It would have been easy for Isaiah to think well of himself, much like the apostle Paul did before he converted. In Philippians 3, Paul boasts an impressive resumé that few could rival, with numerous reasons to confirm his opinion that he was doing better than most. But Paul lost his confidence in his own goodness when he stood in the light of Christ's. He realized that, despite his outstanding credentials, he was never going to be good enough for God on his own. What he formerly had considered to be strengths he now saw as liabilities. His assessment of himself changed when he began with the Lord instead of with himself.

Isaiah also experienced a pivotal turning point in his perspective. He had gone to the temple, quite likely to reflect on the tragic circumstances surrounding King Uzziah's death.[1] Unexpectedly he saw the Lord in all his holiness, seated on his throne attended by heavenly creatures. But this was no beatific vision; it was a moment of truth. For in seeing the Lord clearly, he also saw himself clearly. And he despaired.

Despite all he had going for him personally, politically, and religiously, Isaiah declared, "Woe to me. I am ruined. For I am a man of unclean lips,

---

[1] References taken primarily from Isaiah 6:1-7.

and I live among a people of unclean lips, and my eyes have seen the King, the LORD Almighty."[2] The prophet – the one who spoke the very words of God – was a man whose mouth was not holy. Worse yet, he didn't know it until he stood in the presence of God.

Notice, however, that although he recoiled from what he saw, he didn't recoil from the activity of seeing. Compare his response with King Uzziah's. Uzziah had stood in virtually the same place in the temple and had a similar chance to see himself, but he refused.[3] He had wrongly thought he could take upon himself the duties of a priest. When the true priests challenged him, he got angry with them rather than acknowledge the truth of what they said. God rewarded his stubborn refusal to see correctly by cursing him with leprosy. He fled the temple, his inner uncleanness visibly breaking through his skin in a disease that would take his life.

Uzziah's arrogance and pride sharply contrast with Isaiah's honest self-assessment. Humbly, Isaiah didn't look away. As he stood in God's presence, he could see clearly – and he was willing to look. What a frightening place to be! Naked before the holy gaze of God, utterly exposed, with nowhere to hide. To borrow a picture from J. R. R. Tolkien, he was pinned like a frightened hobbit beneath the penetrating gaze of Sauron's lidless, sleepless eye. No wonder he claims he is ruined. But wait! This is not Sauron's gaze. This is Jehovah's! Infinitely more penetrating and fierce than fiction can imagine, yet infinitely more kind than any writer – or reader – has yet believed. Not only was Isaiah's response different than Uzziah's, God's response to the two men was also different. In his great mercy, God immediately provided atonement. A seraph touched Isaiah's lips with a coal from the altar that removed Isaiah's guilt. Now Isaiah, like Paul, knew righteousness apart from law, apart from his political connections and religious activities. He had seen the Lord, seen himself honestly, and was not destroyed. He had been pardoned.

Isaiah could not have known pardon or mercy without a humble willingness to see himself correctly, but he could not have survived that look without the grace of atonement that followed. God provided both the catalyst that prompted Isaiah to see himself and the safety net so that he could risk looking.

Isaiah had an early taste of what waits for everyone. Jesus tells us that everything we do will be revealed publicly.[4] All our good and evil

---

[2] Isa. 6:5.

[3] 2 Chron. 26:16-23. I am indebted to John Bettler for pointing out the parallels between Isaiah and Uzziah.

[4] Mark 4:22.

will become evident, either now or at the final judgment.[5] We will all have the opportunity to see ourselves for who we truly are, so why not begin the process of humble self-assessment now, before we have to? With a gracious God like Isaiah's and the inevitability of future judgment, why would we resist looking more humbly and honestly at ourselves now?

RESISTANCE TO HUMBLE SELF-ASSESSMENT

A large part of personal ministry involves helping people become more comfortable with assessing themselves. My goal is not to encourage endless introspection but to help someone acknowledge, "This is who I am, and this is what I do." You will struggle to connect with Christ without such self-knowledge because you won't know your true need. Looking at yourself is so necessary, so obvious . . . and so difficult. What holds you back from self-examination? Your resistance, like mine, is rooted in your heart. You either (1) believe you have more to gain by not looking, or (2) you don't believe that Jesus' work on your behalf is enough to deal with what you'll find if you do.

Why should you examine your life if you think you're better off if you don't? Let's try a different question: What do you stand to lose if you admit that you have sinned? Perhaps you'll lose the good opinion of people who are important to you. Or perhaps you're afraid to tarnish your opinion of yourself. Either way, you care more about human opinions than God's. If thinking well of yourself is more important than God's view of you, you cannot afford the cost of self-examination.

I remember giving a friend a hard time when he was trying to show me a place where I was self-absorbed. The details of the conversation escape me, but not the overall tone. I was absolutely committed to not seeing. I didn't want to look. I fought with him, dragging out the conversation until he admitted that perhaps he didn't see clearly either. Only then was I willing to concede that there might be something to what he was saying.

Why was it so hard for me to acknowledge that I might have a problem? It had something to do with measuring myself against him. Because I wanted equal standing in our friendship, I wasn't willing to think honestly about something I had done wrong. I had too much to lose. If I alone was wrong, then I would be less, at least in my eyes and maybe in his. Only when my friend acknowledged a failure of his own could we share the "loss" and maintain the same relationship.

---

[5] 1 Tim. 5:24-25.

Another problem was that I didn't believe that belonging to Christ's family provided any meaningful safety or security for me. I based my worth on my performance and the praise of others. My interaction with my friend was built on that flawed foundation instead of the confident knowledge that my God cared for me no matter what. If, like me, you are tempted to bolster your sense of self-worth with such things, remember how fragile and temporary those supports are. If you lose your abilities through an accident or aging, you lose your self-confidence. One unhappy person can ruin your day. When you build your identity and worth on yourself or others, it doesn't take much to send tremors through your entire edifice.

During Isaiah's lifetime, Israel revolted against its Assyrian overlords and was subsequently besieged.[6] Since it was common knowledge that some in Israel looked to Egypt for military aid, the Assyrian commander attempted to undermine their hopes. Though foolishly boasting of his own might, the commander accurately illustrated the folly of depending on human power to support ourselves. He warned Israel that relying on Egypt was like leaning on a splintered reed: it pierces your hand and wounds you when you put your weight on it.[7] What a picture! By leaning on others, you not only lack support, you've compounded your difficulties by shooting a jagged tube through your hand! The solution, however, is not to find a stronger human to lean on (like Assyria) but to look to your Redeemer.

The only foundation worth having is one you have not created or sustained and, therefore, cannot ruin. Knowing that Jesus loves me because he loves me is not merely a circular argument – it's gloriously circular! Since it begins and ends within the Godhead, my sins and failures cannot threaten the relationship. This is irrationally undesirable to a person bent on developing his own self-worth. It is self-defeating heresy to someone with a "you get out what you put in" work ethic. But it is wonderfully liberating for the person who desires something better than he or she deserves.

Such a foundation allowed a friend of mine to notice her own negative response to a dinner party she was hosting. This woman loved giving parties but found herself responding poorly by the end of the evening. Because she has confidence in Christ's love for her, she quietly began asking herself why she was so sullen and short with her guests. What

---

[6] Thomas L. Constable notes Israel's earlier attempt at building an alliance with Egypt in Isaiah 30:1-5 ("Notes on Isaiah," 2005, published by Sonic Light, http://soniclight.com/constable/notes/pdf/isaiah.pdf, accessed 7/21/05).

[7] Isa. 36:6.

did she want that she wasn't getting? As she examined herself, she realized that she hadn't been complimented for the evening – and she wanted to be! Because she didn't get what she considered her due, she had withdrawn kindness from her guests.

That self-examination took courage. To look at herself when others also needed to face their blindness and thoughtlessness was itself a work of grace. Looking honestly at herself required the courage of humility that says, "Lord, let me see myself and understand why I am doing what I'm doing."

Tasting the Asparagus

But what if your fear of self-examination outweighs your desire? How can you get started? Several years ago my daughter Cassie was having trouble admitting things about herself that seemed obvious to the rest of us.[8] I sat down quietly with her, gave her a hug, and said, "You know, looking at your life when someone points out something wrong is a little like learning to eat vegetables. Nobody likes it. Everyone prefers candy. Candy is easy to like; vegetables are hard to like. But in the long run, vegetables are better for making you strong inside.

"All I want you to do right now is a lot like sticking out your tongue and touching the asparagus to see that it won't hurt you. I don't want you to even think about putting it into your mouth or having to swallow it. I just want you to see that you don't need to be afraid of it. That means you don't have to agree with me about the argument we just had. You don't have to say I was right or prove to me that I was wrong. In fact, I don't even want to talk about this conversation ever again! I just want you to *consider* the *possibility* that it *might* be the case that what we're talking about is a *little* bit true of you."

As she giggled at all my caveats, I continued. "I just want you to touch the asparagus. It's not going to taste like candy. It's not going to make you feel warm and fuzzy inside, like when you do something great at school. But it's good to learn if there might be things about you that need to change. Let's see if you can learn to live just a bit more humbly."

As far as I was concerned, that was the end of the conversation. I simply wanted to introduce the idea that self-examination was a little less horrific than the Spanish Inquisition. But God had a bigger goal and Cassie really took that conversation to heart. The next day at lunch, my

---

8 Thanks to my colleague, Winston Smith, who gave me this illustration, which I shared with my daughter.

wife and I were trying to help one of our sons see an area in *his* life that needed changing. Cassie piped up very matter-of-factly, "Yeah, I do that too." And then, without skipping a beat, she turned to me and said, "See, I'm learning to look at myself!"

What happened that day was an instance of grace: I'm not always that patient, and she's not always that responsive! But that day I was sharing what I had received from Jesus. His sacrifice for me has given me an absolutely rock solid, secure place in his family. Nothing of eternal worth is at risk when I consider my personal sins and flaws. Jesus has set me free and there is no condemnation for me. I have a safe place, guaranteed by God the Father, where I can take a look at myself and see who I really am and how I really affect others without being defensive. Knowing God's heart for me makes such contemplation a safe activity.

Because I have experienced the kind of security that allows me to face who I am, I simply gave my daughter the same kind of security and safety she needed to look at herself. She felt safe with me the way I've felt safe with the Father. But the security I provided Cassie is no substitute for heavenly security, nor is it enough to overcome a person's reluctance to look within. At best it was a signpost showing Cassie what kind of reception she would receive from her heavenly Father. I think she appreciated the signpost, but her willingness to develop a "taste for asparagus" will wane unless she desires real security with the Lord, the ultimate destination, more than what I can offer as the signpost. Apart from grace, none of us would desire or value the destination. Apart from grace, none of us would come to know the security found with him. And apart from grace, none of us would risk taking an honest look at ourselves.

1   Learning to see yourself is hard. To navigate successfully between stubborn
    resistance and ruinous self-loathing, you need a clear sense of your place
    with Christ. This would be a good time to review earlier chapters on
    God's commitment to you.

2   Often we are selectively blind: our most frequent failings don't fit our
    ideal image of ourselves, so we get used to ignoring them. What is your
    preferred picture of yourself? How might that picture make it harder to
    see yourself accurately?

3   When I consider doing something I dread, I find it helpful to list the positive
    reasons to do it. What are some godly reasons to evaluate the negatives
    of your life?

4   Sometimes negative results can create positive motivation. Think about
    some of the consequences you've experienced when you haven't taken
    a more honest look at yourself. Write them down as a warning against
    too quickly excusing yourself in the future.

Are you getting better at confessing your faults?

Once you're willing to take an honest look at yourself, what logically follows is admitting what you've discovered. When you realize how hard it is for people to honestly acknowledge who they are and what they've done, you can see that taking this next step is powerful evidence that God is working in them. Reality court TV offers a glimpse into how much difficulty people have in confessing simple truths.

HONESTY: THE BEST OF ALL THE LOST ARTS

A typical segment begins with the plaintiff explaining her suit to the judge. "My boyfriend's been cheating on me. I threw him out and he won't pay back the $3,000 I loaned him." The judge will then ask the boyfriend, "Is this true?" Not once does the guy say, "Yeah. She's right, I was a jerk and I owe her the money. I just don't want to give it back." Instead you'll hear something like, "Oh no, Your Honor. The money was a gift." The judge will then ask, "The money was a gift, but were you cheating on her?"

"Well, it wasn't really cheating. She wasn't always home so I liked to go out with a few friends."

"And were these guy friends or girl friends?"

"Oh . . . they were kind of both."

"They were both. And did you go out with them both together?"

"Um, well . . . no."

"So you went out on dates with girls by yourself while you already had a girlfriend."

"Well, yeah, I guess."

Now the judge, barely holding onto his patience, sums up, "Then can you help me understand how going out with other girls by yourself while you have a girlfriend is not cheating?"

I could go on, but you get the point – and we haven't even gotten to the $3,000 yet! Such conversations are long and circuitous; the only thing they make clear is that confession and repentance are not our first impulse. If they were, court TV would be much less interesting. We are innately deceitful. Have you noticed that children don't need to be taught to lie? I have never had to say to my kids, "Listen, there are going to be times in your life when you will want to deceive someone and I want to make sure you're good at it." Instead, like you and me, my kids were born experts!

Court TV also reminds me why I don't want to be a judge. I suspect that judges feel the same way at times. I wouldn't be surprised if Samuel, one of Israel's most honored judges, felt that way after his ordeal confronting Saul.[1] God had commanded Saul to destroy the Amalekites along with all their possessions. Saul was to spare nothing, fulfilling God's vow to avenge Amalek's mistreatment of Israel when God brought them out of Egypt. But Saul disobeyed: he let Agag, the king, live and he allowed his army to keep the best of the Amalekite plunder, only destroying what was considered worthless.

Here again is a glimpse of our magnificent God. Saul was in desperate trouble and didn't know it. He just had been commanded to destroy a nation that had earlier opposed God's purposes. He didn't see, however, that in his disobedience, he also opposed God. He had put himself in Amalek's place and didn't realize it. God gave a clear instruction that Saul blatantly disobeyed, but God in his mercy sent his prophet Samuel to help Saul see more clearly. When God confronts you, he is loving you. He's helping you when you aren't even aware that you need help. In giving Saul an opportunity to acknowledge what he had done, God gave him grace.

Unfortunately, Saul rejected that grace. He turned what should have been a fairly easy conversation – "Yes, Samuel, I disobeyed" – into a fiasco by repeatedly refusing to admit what he'd done. From one perspective, you can read this story as a case study in how not to respond when you're confronted.

A TALE OF TWO KINGS

Saul initiated the conversation with Samuel by proclaiming that he had done everything God told him to do.[2] The irony is powerful: God sent Samuel to talk to Saul about his deficiencies in obedience, and Saul began by telling Samuel how well he had obeyed. Not a promising start!

---

[1] 1 Sam. 15:1-35.
[2] 1 Sam. 15:13.

When Samuel arrives to confront Saul,[3] he immediately notices that live-stock from the conquest had been spared. Yet Saul brazenly declares his obedience. Are you amazed at Saul's nerve? Can you relate to him? Are there times when you know you've done wrong, yet you proclaim your innocence? When God's messengers come to you, do you start by telling them how good you are?

This gospel-fighter – the desire to proclaim our own righteousness in the face of indisputable evidence – lodges deep within our souls. If we are to be people who gladly and freely repent, we've got to stop believing that we are innocent until proven guilty. The hard reality of the cross should remind us that we are not generally good, and we are certainly not innocent. Instead of a great defense to shore up our self-righteousness, we need the humility that comes from recognizing we are utterly dependent on Christ's righteousness. As we rely more on what Jesus has done for us, we have less need to trumpet our perfections. We won't need to assert our goodness as though our lives depended on it – especially when it's obvious that we have disobeyed.

After Saul's self-serving greeting, Samuel refuted Saul's declaration of obedience by asking why he could hear sheep and oxen if everything had been destroyed. Instead of acknowledging that he had disobeyed, Saul brazenly tried to redefine the livestock that gave him away. He took undeniable facts that condemned him and spun them: "These are not animals wrongly gained by ignoring God. They are 'sacrifices' to honor God."[4] By introducing religious talk, Saul took something terribly straightforward – his disobedience – and made it murky. He even expected Samuel to accept his explanation and agree that he had obeyed the Lord. But in his attempt to disguise his disobedience as obedience, he only deceived himself.

Samuel tried again, telling Saul what God had told him regarding Saul's disobedience.[5] This time Saul was willing to admit that some wrong had been done, but not by him; it was the soldiers. He blame-shifted. Blame-shifting is another skill you don't have to teach kids, but it truly blossoms when adults employ it. A wife might say something like, "I only got angry because he came home and insulted me!" The husband, not willing to be outdone, will reply, "If she'd clean the bathroom every now and then, I wouldn't insult her!" Both are to blame and yet both feel completely justified in blaming the other. So few of us readily admit,

---

[3] 1 Sam. 15:14.
[4] 1 Sam. 15:15.
[5] 1 Sam. 15:18-19.

"I'm responsible for this rotten thing," when someone else could be saddled with it.

Samuel confronted Saul one last time and, with his back against the wall, Saul finally acknowledged that he sinned because he feared his people.[6] Finally, the real problem is revealed. Saul was worried about what other people might think, so he gave in to their wishes. No wonder he couldn't come clean! He was the king. He was supposed to be the leader, but he turned out to be ruled by his people. Hiding his sin made sense in light of his desire not to appear weak. Hiding his sin made sense given what he wanted in life. But not all kings suffer from the same afflictions. The contrast between Saul and David, Israel's second king, could not be more striking.

Whenever David finally saw his sin – whether it was his adultery with Bathsheba, the murder of her husband, or his proud reliance on military might to protect Israel rather than the Lord – he quickly confessed.[7] His conscience worked properly since it was in tune with God and God's view of the world. Granted, it was a little slow: we would prefer that he had seen sin coming and hated it when he was still being tempted. But what an amazing thing that he saw his sin at all!

It is hard to see sin for what it is. Our world blurs the distinctions between sin and holiness constantly. It is easy to make excuses for what we've done. That's why it is refreshing to see David simply own his faults. Not only does he confess what he's done, he fully accepts the blame. He doesn't try to evade responsibility or shift it to someone else. He doesn't minimize what he's done. He takes responsibility for his sin. He (eventually) seizes each opportunity God provides. This is not to say that David is a good guy. His life is dotted with many huge failures – among them adultery, deceit, and murder. When he took a census of his soldiers, 70,000 Israelites died before David was willing to be held solely responsible for his sin.[8] But he is a man who understands his sinfulness. He realizes what he's done and it bothers him.

Both kings are monstrous in the ways they sin, although David might actually be the worse of the two. What separates them is their responses: one tries to cover his sin while the other clearly admits his fault. These radically different responses reveal radically different relationships with God. When Saul spoke of God to Samuel, he repeatedly said, "your God," even as he planned to go worship him. *Your* God, three times – it

---

6 1 Sam. 15:24.

7 2 Sam. 11-12; 2 Sam. 24.

8 My thanks to Sue Lutz for this insight.

stands out like a sore thumb. At best Saul was indicating an impersonal relationship with God. At worst, he was tacitly admitting a rejection of the God who set him on the throne of Israel.

David, on the other hand, spoke personally of God. Psalm 51, believed to be written by David after his sin with Bathsheba, is a very personal address that demonstrates intimate knowledge of his Lord. In fact, his knowledge of God is what allowed him to confess in the first place. Often we read Psalm 51 as a model of how to repent: here's what to say to God; here's what you need to see about your life; here are the steps of repentance. But underlying all the how-to information is a richness of what to believe about your God in order to repent well. Let's take a moment to work through the psalm, asking, "What does David know about God that I need to know to confess my sins?"

In verse 1, for example, David asks for mercy according to God's steadfast love. God first revealed that aspect of his nature to Moses on Mount Sinai, immediately after Israel had worshiped the golden calf.[9] Poured into the phrase "steadfast love" are all the ways God related to his people: he heard their cries in slavery, rescued them, provided for them, and was about to pardon their idolatry. In reflecting on his sins, David says, "I need mercy in keeping with that kind of God. What I've done is so big that a smaller god will not suffice. I need to approach a God whose patience and mercy can handle what I've done." Given the scope of what he's done, anything short of steadfast love would not be enough for forgiveness. As you walk through the psalm asking this same question, you will see a God David could trust; a God to whom he was willing to admit his sins and failings.

Because he had confidence, David ran to God, confessing his failures and receiving mercy. He was disciplined by God, but he regained peace with him. If you don't think peace with God is terribly important, ask Saul. In his interaction with Samuel, he learned that he was no longer God's appointed king. That was bad, but what was worse was that he lost peace with God. In earlier days, Saul had had his heart changed by God.[10] God had sent his Spirit upon him so that he prophesied. After the confrontation with Samuel, however, the spirit God sent was an evil one that tormented Saul.[11] Saul knew how marvelous peace with God was because he knew what it was to experience its absence.[12]

---

9 Ex. 34:6-7.
10 1 Sam. 10:9-13.
11 1 Sam. 16:14-16.
12 1 Sam. 18:12.

Since you can't ask Saul, ask someone who knows what it is like to be jolted awake at 2:00 A.M. by anxieties running riot through his brain; someone who can't go back to sleep amid the flood of fears and accusations. Peace with God is a blessing not to be compared.

HIDERS VS. CONFESSORS

Not only does confession of sin restore peace with God, it also restores peace between people. By contrast, covering up sin ensures ruined relationships. Which would make you more angry as a parent: your daughter lying about attending an unchaperoned party or the fact that she went? Certainly, you would be upset that she went somewhere she knew you would not approve, but her attempted deception strikes at the root of your relationship. This is true of deception in all relationships. It always compounds the problem by ruining the relationship.

For several years, I was the business manager for a thrift store run by a Christian organization. Part of my job involved counting each day's receipts and reconciling the cash drawer with the register tape. Many times there were small discrepancies between the two that were easily rectified. But for a two-month stretch, large sums of money were missing with no way to account for them. The cashiers had been with the store for years and we'd never had this problem, yet every few days another incident occurred. I came to dread reconciling the drawer. Everyone was questioned and blamed, and all those with access to the drawer lived under a cloud of suspicion.

Eventually we caught the person responsible. It was someone we all had considered above suspicion. He had avoided detection primarily because he had our complete confidence. For two months he had lied to us, covering up what he was doing. When we finally got to the bottom of things, we learned that his life had been veering badly out of control for quite awhile, but he'd never said a word about it. Having his problems exposed was clearly God's mercy to him. But because he had to get caught before he was willing to confess, I never fully trusted him again. Deceitfulness always destroys friendships. Conversely – and ironically – people who tell their friends how they've wronged them develop stronger friendships.

I have been privileged to have several friends come to me at different times and say, "Do you remember the other day? Well, what I did was wrong and I want to apologize." Often I have not been as upset as the other person about the matter; sometimes I was not even aware of it. But my friends, sensitized by the Holy Spirit, couldn't live with themselves until they made things right.

Those are special moments of grace that move good friends even closer. Those are people I trust even though they have sinned against me. I see how they respond to the Spirit's promptings. They are not at peace with sin or its corrosive effects on friendship, so they work to remove it. For them the biggest problem with sin is not the embarrassment it causes but the relational ruin it produces (including their relationship with God). They are people I trust.

DOING THE MATH

You may feel yourself caught at this point. You know that a failure to confess your sins will ruin your relationships with God and others. You believe that God will receive you and that life will truly be better, yet you struggle to acknowledge the truth when someone confronts you. You find it difficult to admit to the things about yourself that aren't good. You believe well but live poorly. One of my colleagues has very wisely said, "When there are times in your life where your theology lines up in one place, but your actions are completely contrary, always choose to believe your life, not your theology."[13] In other words, you always live out your real faith, even if it's different from what you would say on a theology exam or in a Sunday school class. If you say you believe God is merciful and that you are secure in him, yet you are reluctant to repent when you have wronged someone, the reality is that some other belief controls you. How can you change so that your life theology lines up with Scripture? How do you change your desires so that you want what God wants more than what your unredeemed nature wants? You do what another colleague, Tim Lane, following Martin Luther,[14] calls "doing the math."

When your motivations are out of whack and you love the wrong things more than you love Christ, take a step back and look at what you love – respect, honor, reputation – and compare it with Jesus. Ask:

- Respect, when have you ever done anything for me?
- When have you cared for me and worked hard to help me?
- When have you given of yourself so that I might be better off?

---

13 This is only one of the many things I've gleaned from Ed Welch's comments over the years.

14 In his preface to his *Commentary on the Epistle to the Galatians* (Grand Rapids: Zondervan, 1949), Luther addresses the law ("O law!") as a usurper of the loyalties of his heart and life that rightly belong to the gospel. Lane's "doing the math" adapts the model Luther developed.

- When have you promised to help me, to be with me forever? Have you ever promised never to leave me or forsake me?
- Did you ever leave the throne where I have worshiped you, come down and die for me that I might live instead?
- Where have you ever aided me when I was stuck, lost, in doubt, in trouble, or ruining relationships?

Then you ask Jesus the exact same questions and compare the results. You do the math.

This is not difficult. My daughter was seven when she listened to a sermon in which Tim urged us to do the math. A few days later she was captivated by an advertisement in a book catalog. Over the course of an hour, she repeatedly announced her desire for specific books that caught her eye. As it became apparent that the only sound she was hearing was the siren song of advertising, I suggested that something had captured her attention more than Jesus. She paused, looked at me, and said, "I guess I need to do the math. Catalog books, when did you ever die for me? What have you ever done for me?" As she walked out of the room, that was the last we heard of the book sale . . . at least for that day. My daughter saw where her desires did not line up with Christ's, and she did something to realign herself.

If you know you have been welcomed into a safe place with God the Father where you will never be condemned, you will welcome people speaking into your life. You will freely admit your sins. You won't be shocked by the reality of being a sinner and feel driven to run, hide, or deceive. Instead, knowing how good you're not, you'll focus on the grace and kindness of Christ. You will prize the joy that comes from having peace with God and with your friends. And you won't risk losing that joy for the little embarrassment that admitting your sins might generate.

on your own

1   Think of a time in the last day or two when you rejected an opportunity
     to confess your sin. Make a list of the Saul-like strategies you fall into
     most easily.

2   Now spend some time processing that list with the Lord. Prayerfully ask,
     "What was so important to me that it blinded me to what you wanted me
     to see?" Ask his forgiveness for your failure to repent. Thank him for giv-
     ing you the chance to see yourself and ask him for another.

3   Look carefully today for that next opportunity. Whom has Jesus used in the
     past to bring such messages to your heart? Whom are you most likely to
     hear? Whom do you have the most trouble hearing?

4   How might you respond thoughtfully instead of automatically defending
     yourself and denying your friend's concerns? Give careful thought to
     what you must not let yourself say. What could you say that would be
     of more value?

Are you learning to open up your life to others?

So far, we've been talking about ways that God changes us, enabling us to see our problems and confess our faults. These changes keep us from ruining relationships, both with God and with others. In that sense, they're preventative. But God's work in us always goes beyond that, moving us outward toward praising him and helping people. Surprising as it may be, he so thoroughly redeems us that even our failures can bring him glory and benefit his people. Paul the apostle was very familiar with such radical redemption. Far from being embarrassed by his past, he regularly dredged it up, publicly discussing his failures.[1]

At first, that seems a little strange. It's one thing to confess your sins at the time you committed them; it's another to keep drawing attention to sins from the past. Why would you want to remind people of how bad you were? If God remembers our sins no more, why does Paul keep them in mind? It seems even stranger given our assumptions about preachers. Aren't preachers like Paul supposed to be positive role models, pointing us to what is right? It almost seems counterproductive for Paul to talk about the ways he had sinned. Can you think of another occupation that emphasizes its past failures?

Suppose you were thumbing through the Yellow Pages and came across a restaurant ad that claimed, "We used to burn food and poison our customers, but that was last year. Come try us now!" How quickly would you grab your phone to make reservations? Or what about a plumber advertising, "I used to break sinks, but I'm a lot better now. Let me come over and work on yours!" Such claims don't inspire much confidence. They're truthful but unlikely to garner much business.

---

[1] Acts 22:3-5; Gal. 1:13; Phil. 3:6; 1 Cor. 15:9; 1 Tim. 1:15-16.

Yet that's what Paul does. He tells you, "I used to persecute the church, but now I preach the gospel." Just like the early Christians in Acts, you're tempted to think, *Not in my church you're not!* Paul takes aspects of his life that seem better left forgotten and regularly puts them on display. Why? When Paul talks about his past, he reminds you that being the "worst of sinners" includes being a blasphemer, a persecutor, and an enemy of Jesus.[2] Yet he says he received mercy so that Christ's patience with him would be an example to others who seek him. Paul says that his public confessions serve two ends: they give glory to God and hope to others.

Just as Before and After photos show you the effect of an exercise program, cosmetic surgery, or a weight loss drug, Paul's history shows the effect that Jesus has had in his life. He doesn't mind highlighting what he was before Jesus changed him because in so doing he highlights Jesus' glory. You can't miss the brilliant diamonds of God's patience when displayed against the dark velvet of Paul's former life. Far from being a press-hungry celebrity reveling in his degradation, hungry for any and all attention, Paul talks about his past sins because he longs to draw your attention to Jesus.

Confessing his sins also provides hope to other people. If Paul had merely been a nice man when he converted to Christianity, his testimony would not give as much hope to people who had sinned flagrantly. But this way, people who are unsure whether Jesus will receive them can compare themselves with Paul, a deceived, self-righteous, violent murderer who disguised his activities with religious trappings. If Jesus could save Paul, he can do the same for them. Paul's confession inspires others with hope.

Because Paul knows he's accepted by God for Christ's sake, he doesn't need to make himself look better than he is. He can look beyond self-interest and be concerned for a larger world. In this manner, Paul lives out Jesus' two great commandments – love God and love your neighbor – in the way he deals with his past. He demonstrates that you are willing to talk about your failings if your goal is to demonstrate the greatness of God's glory and to help other people.

LOVE FOR GOD AND NEIGHBOR . . . OR FOR SELF?

In the previous chapter, we noticed how consumed King Saul was with protecting his reputation. If you continue studying his life, you'll discover that he was also greatly concerned with his own honor and

---

2 1 Tim. 1:12-17.

glory. He set up a monument to himself after the battle with Amalek, he wanted Samuel to worship with him so that he would be honored by the elders of Israel, and he never gave up his longing to establish a dynasty even after God rejected him as king.[3] Saul's longing for honor didn't allow him to confess his sins when Samuel confronted him. Driven by his desire for glory, how could he admit to Samuel, to God – or even to himself – that he had done anything wrong? When you yearn for glory, admitting failure only hurts your cause.

Unfortunately, Saul is not alone in being a glory hog. Other people in Scripture declined to confess their shortcomings because they too desired unblemished reputations above all else. Ananias and Sapphira, wanting to appear as generous as other believers, lied about how much of their income they were giving to the early church.[4] Knowing the truth, Peter asked each of them separately to speak honestly, but they both refused. Elisha's servant, Gehazi, wrongly extorted payment from Naaman the Aramean, whom Elisha had healed of leprosy.[5] He then hid what he'd taken and tried to hide the truth from Elisha. Notice God's kindness here. In both cases, God gave each person an opportunity to confess his sin and choose God's glory over his own. Yet each turned down his invitation, believing that deception would protect his reputation. They went on to receive God's severe punishment.

Think about your own life. Where do you yearn to establish your own glory or long for others to recognize your achievements? Do you need people – or do you need yourself – to think that you have a successful career? That you are a good mom or a loving husband? A responsible homemaker? An obedient child? A model Christian who reads her Bible daily and always loves attending small group? If success in any area controls you, you will find it next to impossible to admit when you fail. You will not use your sins, past or present, to praise Christ or help others. Instead, you will bury your harsh outbursts, your critical and cold exchanges with your wife, your financial irresponsibility, and addictive patterns. When you are consumed with maintaining an ideal image, it is impossible to talk about the way God has redeemed your sins and failures.

With this façade, you will be of little help to others. You'll either be too lofty for the rest of us to imitate, or you'll lose credibility as we simply won't believe that you always do the right thing! Either way, you'll have little to say to those of us who struggle to be faithful in our daily living.

---

[3] 1 Sam. 15:12, 30; 18:5-9; 20:30-31.
[4] Acts 5:1-11.
[5] 2 Kings 5:19-27.

INTO THE LIGHT

Talking about my failings is not something I've always found easy. By nature and training, I am insecure and hypersensitive. I have worked hard at projecting an image of someone with all the right answers and a life that backs them up. Obviously, that fiction has never been true. I am just as weak and rebellious as anyone else. Yet I've clung to that image in the hope that it would bring me the respect I craved.

I remember being amazed when I started attending a church where the pastors regularly talked about their own sins and failings. This was bad for my image-building agenda but good for my soul. I wondered, *How do you get the grace to admit those things to anyone, much less announce them publicly?!* Here were people who talked from a podium through loudspeakers about things I wouldn't whisper privately. This not only amazed me, it helped me.

I learned how to interact better with God and other people. Through my pastors' confessions, I learned that life doesn't end when my image cracks. Instead, the cracks can be the beginning of a life of real integrity, of honestly relating to others on the basis of grace, not on an ideal and imaginary image. My pastors demonstrated the value of confessing sins for the benefit of others, but I needed to learn it by experience. Although slow and painful, it is well worth the trouble. I've seen my own family benefit as I grow more transparent about my shortcomings.

The other day I was standing at our back door watching my two sons play together. It appeared that my older son had tricked his younger brother into ducking down so that he could bounce a ball off his head. As I stood there holding my coffee cup, I tried to convince myself, *I didn't just see that.* I've been trying to develop the patience of being slow to anger and not jumping to evil conclusions about others, so I did nothing, hoping that I was mistaken. Then he did it again.

He had beaned his brother twice now – that is, twice that I'd seen – but I decided that perhaps patience was the better course of action. I clutched my cup more tightly, hoping that at any moment his conscience – which all orthodox theologians declare he has – would kick in and he'd decide that there were better uses for his brother's skull. Unfortunately, my hope proved to be groundless as he did it one more time.

At that point, my patience ended and my temper went from zero to sixty in an instant. With intimidation in my heart, I jerked open the door and, in my most sanctified and Christian manner, bellowed, "BOY! Get in this house." I marched him into a back room, absolutely livid. Having been picked on by others myself, I was incensed to see my son bullying another.

I began to lay into him verbally with a long list of what he'd been doing out there. I asked questions to which there can be no good response: "You're a real big man to pick on a two-year-old, aren't you?!" I was mercilessly sarcastic in my assessment of his character. (On my more pessimistic days I wonder if the primary skill I have learned as a counselor is how to sin more effectively against my family.)

My son responded to my anger by evading the issue with every deceptive device at his disposal. He pretended ignorance. He didn't volunteer any information, waiting to see what I knew and what I didn't. He avoided eye contact, stared at the floor, the walls, my shirt – anything to avoid my furious gaze.

Now I was even more enraged. I found myself thinking things that I wished would not flash through my mind. I was tempted to hurt him. I wanted him to feel the injustice of what I had just seen him do. I started to rationalize silently, *Well, maybe if he experiences what he just did to his brother, it will teach him not to do it again.* Then, like a flash, I realized that I was tempted to do exactly what he did! I was longing to bully him in the same way he was bullying his little brother. I thank God for giving me a conscience and his Holy Spirit! Otherwise, I would completely ruin all of my relationships, including this one with my son. The truth that my son and I are pretty much the same person began to seep in around the edges of my anger.

My rage began to deflate. The Holy Spirit stepped in more aggressively and suggested that there might be a more redemptive way to deal with my wayward son. Then I remembered one day in elementary school when I repeatedly hurt a smaller boy. I deflated some more. I remembered how intoxicating the taste of misused power can be – how you both hate what you're doing and feed on it at the same time. Now my ungodly anger was flat. I began telling him about that time when I was younger. Instead of silently enduring my diatribe, he began asking me questions.

I have seen this dynamic at work repeatedly with my children. When I begin to confess how my sins are just like theirs, little heads pick up. The rug pattern becomes much less interesting and they begin to participate in the conversation. They realize we are basically the same and that if there's hope for Dad after the horrible things he's done, then there's certainly hope for them. That glimmer of hope I see in them is what has encouraged me to keep opening up. As long as protecting myself remains my primary goal, I won't talk about anything I've done wrong. But as soon as helping people grow in their faith becomes more important than protecting my reputation, I become willing to open my life to whatever extent is helpful. Paul exposed his life to help others and taught others to do the same. Other people taught me and now I teach others as well.

The same dynamic plays out in personal ministry. Confessing my failings to people who come looking for help makes me more approachable when I'm counseling or discipling. People know that I truly understand the need for mercy, which gives them hope that I will treat them mercifully. They feel emboldened to confront their problems instead of hiding or minimizing them. They begin talking about where they've been and what they've done.

In a context of mercy, confessing sin is contagious. Doing so draws sinners closer to Christ, and it purifies his church as people expose what is going on in their hearts and lives. Confessing your sins to others gives them permission to confess their own. It's a good thing to have sin out in the open where it can be dealt with, rather than hidden where it festers. People who know God become people who not only examine themselves and confess their failings, they also speak freely of their past to honor God and to serve his people.

Two months after I taught a Sunday school class, I ran into a man who had attended. He reminded me that I had confessed to a temptation I have at work to "quietly twist arms in back rooms" to accomplish my agenda. He talked about how those comments had helped him see himself more accurately and helped him repent. Two months! I have trouble remembering things I heard two days ago. What grabbed his attention is what grabbed mine when my pastors spoke of their failures. He saw his ugliness more clearly yet had more hope that Jesus would receive and purify him. Do you want Jesus to have that effect on other people through you? He's willing – longing! – to do so. It begins with your motivation: for whose glory are you living?

on your own

1 The way you tell (or don't tell) your story speaks volumes about what you really believe. You declare how much you trust and value Christ's love for you every time you talk about where you've been and what you've done. Think for a moment about what you tell people about your life when you're getting to know them. Do you casually wallow in past sins ("I was so drunk that . . ."), skip over them out of embarrassment ("I was born on a little farm in Kansas and now here I am"), or do you point out the ways Jesus has changed you? Most of us need to repent of being more concerned with ourselves than with God's plans to use our lives to build his church for his glory.

2 Can you recall a time when you risked sharing with a friend how the Lord had worked in your life through your faults? Think about the effect your disclosure had on the other person. How did he or she respond? What did he or she learn?

3 List two or three areas in your life that Jesus has been addressing lately. Now make a list of your friends, family, and coworkers. Which of them would benefit from hearing how Jesus has been at work? How could you use his present activities to bring hope to someone else?

4 Ask God to help you recognize opportunities to use your life to help someone else by "bragging" about what he has done for you.

Are you learning to forgive?

Learning to confess your sins more freely leads you to ask forgiveness from God and the people you have wronged. Actually experiencing that forgiveness, however, is nothing short of amazing! Do you recall the nearly physical relief you felt the last time someone forgave you? The weight that lifted from your shoulders? Giving and receiving forgiveness are hallmarks of the Christian life.[1] They are the ways in which the community of faith deals with our sins against each other.[2] But that doesn't make forgiveness easy. Peter wrestles with this in Matthew 18:21 when he asks Jesus, "Lord, how many times shall I forgive my brother when he sins against me? Up to seven times?" Our first impulse is to laugh at him. "Oh, Peter. You don't know anything about mercy. Seven times? Why, everybody knows it's much closer to seventy times seven!" We laugh, but *does* everybody know what forgiveness means and what it demands?

WHEN SEVEN FEELS LIKE INFINITY

Jesus set Peter straight, but he didn't laugh. He knew that forgiving others is not easy. Let's say you are a young woman looking forward to a special date. You've been thinking about your boyfriend since you went to sleep last night and you have conservatively spent 3.2 hours getting ready. But he doesn't show up on time. Being a charitable person, you don't mind him being a little late – actually you used the extra time for those last-minute finishing touches! But after fifteen minutes, you start to wonder where he is. After twenty-five minutes, you're getting a bit irritated. This grows in intensity every five minutes or so until he's fifty minutes late. Now, irritation morphs into anxiety as you start to

---

[1] Matt. 18:21-35.
[2] 2 Cor. 2:7; Col. 3:13.

worry that he might have been in an accident. Finally, he rolls in about an hour late and says, "Oh, sorry. I just really wanted to finish the project I was working on at the office. I should have called. Please forgive me." And you do.

The next week, he does the same thing. This time you're a little quicker to notice and a little less lenient about the time. But you're also much more worried because surely, after last week, something really bad must have happened for him to be late this time. But again nothing serious took place – he just wanted to finish watching the game. No big deal; he simply took you for granted again. When he asks you to forgive him this time, it's a little harder to muster up the desire (the man has a cell phone, after all), but you do.

Several weeks later he does it again. He doesn't have a good reason . . . again. He asks you to forgive him, again. This time it's even harder to forgive, and we're only up to three times. The fourth time he asks forgiveness, you explode. "No! I don't want to forgive you because you're obviously not taking this seriously. No one can be that clueless!" He asks you to believe that, yes, some people really are. And so it goes. You get the point: forgiving someone seven times for the same thing is no small achievement. (I should note for the record that men can offer plenty of examples where women try them in similar ways. This is not a gender-based problem!)

Seven is starting to feel like a stretch. Please recognize that we're not even talking about difficult things like someone deceiving you, stealing from you, or slandering you. Forgiving others is hard work! Bitterness and avoidance come much more easily to us.

A Forgiving Man Is Hard to Find

Here's a challenge for you. Put this book down for thirty seconds and try to list all the great forgivers in the Bible. It's hard to come up with many. Can you remember any? If I'd asked you to select a villain, you'd have had no problem. You can also find numerous exemplars of courage, faithfulness, shrewdness, and service. But great forgivers are hard to find.

David seemed to demonstrate forgiveness during his exile. After being cursed by Shimei, one of Saul's relatives,[3] David didn't allow his men to kill the mocker. He even pardoned Shimei when he re-ascended his throne.[4] But when he later charged his son Solomon not to allow

---

[3] 2 Sam. 16:5-14.
[4] 2 Sam. 19:14-23.

Shimei to die from old age, it's clear that there had been no forgiveness, just delayed judgment.[5] Another example of forgiveness, a beautiful example that quickly comes to mind, is the father of the Prodigal Son.[6] But he is a fictional character who represents God the Father, not a human being.

As you search the Scriptures for models of forgiveness, you slowly begin to realize that, not only is God the biggest and best, he's one of the very few. Collectively we human beings are pretty bad at forgiveness. This realization should lead you to spend a few moments repenting because, chances are, you're bad at forgiving too. Just think about today and all the people who have irritated you: the driver who cut you off, the coworker who took credit for your work, the child who interrupts every phone conversation. How easy has it been today to forgive these minor infractions and receive people with open arms? Forgiving is critically important, but it's hard to do and hard to find trailblazers who will show us the path.

What do you look for in a forgiving person? If David's dealings with Shimei teach you anything about forgiveness, it's that words alone are not enough. Have you ever had someone say he forgives you, only to learn later from his actions that he really hasn't? A moment of absolution is insufficient; you need an ongoing forgiving attitude. It's a little bit like doing high energy particle physics. (Trust me on this!) You cannot actually see the particle you're studying by looking directly at it; it's too small. Instead, you look for evidence of its existence: its trail on a photographic plate shows how the particle behaved when it encountered other particles.

What does the evidence of a forgiving attitude look like? What trail does it leave? We should look for someone who is patient and longsuffering with people who have wronged him. Someone who continues doing good to others, looking out for their best interests. Someone who, when insulted or sinned against, doesn't react by protecting himself, retaliating, or shutting down. We're looking for someone who extends mercy over the long haul to those who make his or her life difficult. In short, forgiving others looks a lot like 1 Corinthians 13's description of what it means to love someone. As you read that passage, you realize that love takes a long-term approach to difficult relationships. And you also realize that's how the apostle Paul treated difficult people.

---

[5] 1 Kings 2:8-9.
[6] Luke 15:11-32.

PAUL: PATIENT UNDER FIRE

Paul had plenty of opportunities to practice forgiving others because of the many ways people sinned against him, and he took advantage of those opportunities. When illegally beaten by the Philippian magistrates and imprisoned by the jailer, Paul didn't sink into self-pity or bitterness. He turned his attention to saving the jailer's life and then his soul.[7] When he returned to Jerusalem, some men stirred up a mob that seized him.[8] After the crowd dragged him from the temple, beat him, and had him bound with chains, Paul asked if he could speak to them. That is not the request of someone nursing a grudge; it comes from someone intent on winning over his opposition.

Governor Felix kept Paul in prison for two years hoping for a bribe, and again Paul did not spend his time bemoaning his fate.[9] Instead, he wrote letters to instruct the faithful, evangelized the guards, and encouraged those around him. When people tried to make trouble for him, he was grateful that God's purposes in proclaiming the gospel continued.[10] When showed disrespect by the Corinthians, he responded by trying to win them over, not for his own sake, but for theirs. He entreated them gently. He tried to win back their affection, which they should have graciously and unstintingly[11] given him. Apparently he gave Mark a second chance to serve with him even though Mark had abandoned an earlier missions trip.[12]

Paul's life demonstrated an open-hearted attitude toward those who opposed him and sinned against him. He knew how to cancel a debt and let it go rather than brood on it. Not only did he write "the love chapter" in 1 Corinthians, he lived it. He is very much like Joseph, whose actions demonstrated that he had truly pardoned his brothers for their crime against him.[13] But, unlike Joseph, we know something of Paul's former lifestyle. We know that he didn't always handle opposition with grace.

As a devout Pharisee, Paul saw Christianity as a heretical threat to Judaism. From his perspective, Christians were dangerous to his religion. He reacted by violently censoring them. He approved the death of Stephen, a Christian leader, and then set off to destroy the young church, arresting both men and women.[14] Not content to restrict his

---

[7] Acts 16:16-34.
[8] Acts 21:27-39.
[9] Acts 24:26-27.
[10] Phil. 1:15-18.
[11] 2 Cor. 6:11-13 and chapters 10-13.
[12] Acts 15:36-41; 2 Tim. 4:11.
[13] Gen. 50:15-21.

activities to Jerusalem, he extended his reach to arrest and punish Christians from Damascus. In his own words, he persecuted Christians to death.[15]

Keep in mind that the Christians hadn't actually done anything to him. Their "sin" was a figment of his imagination. In that light, his extreme and violent reaction is even more appalling. Clearly, Paul was not used to forgiving those who sinned against him. There is no evidence of it in his words or actions. When he was opposed, Paul was a man of little charity.

Paul's pre-Christian history demonstrated that he was not simply a naturally peace-loving man who carried this quality into his Christian life. Yet, as a Christian, he handled difficult people and situations (true opposition, not simply perceived opposition) with longsuffering, indicating an underlying posture of forgiveness. He didn't ignore the difficulties these people generated, but he didn't turn against the people who caused them. How did he change so much? He learned from the way Jesus treated him.

Though Paul didn't realize it, he had become God's enemy when he fought against the church. Now God needed to deal with Paul, the man who, in pursuing "heretics," had become the true opposition to God and his plans. If he had treated Paul the way Paul had treated the followers of Christ, God would have breathed out murderous threats against Paul. He would have detained, arrested, and imprisoned Paul against his will. He would have punished Paul, hounded him, and stood by, approving of his death. It was God's turn to forcibly suppress Paul, but God didn't take his turn.

Instead, he befriended him.[16] God spoke with him so he could see his errors. He bound him with blindness that forced him to give up his crusade against the church. The blindness protected God's people but also blessed Paul by restraining him from further evil and showing him how spiritually blind he had been. It was a gracious binding to which God also sent a gracious relief. God gave his former enemy back his sight. He transformed Paul so radically that his name had to change – from Saul to Paul – to mark his life's new direction. In short, Jesus was gracious to his opposition: he forgave Paul and treated him as a friend.

---

14 Acts 8:1-3.
15 Acts 22:4-5.
16 Acts 9:1-19.

In response, Paul became gracious to those who later opposed and hindered him. Paul became what he had experienced.

The point is that Jesus does not expect Paul – or you – to create godliness out of thin air. He does not give you an impersonal example to emulate, like some mythic Greek hero whose beauty and bravery you idolize but have not experienced. Impersonal examples can be powerful; that's why we read biographies of noteworthy men and women. But the things we experience have a far greater impact because they can actually change who we are.

Nick and Claire delight in giving scholarships to help others further their education. They want to help people who are striving to better themselves. But this is not an abstract do-good thing for them. They are the first people in both their families to attend college. They were only able to do this because they were helped along the way. They experienced the grace and kindness of others and now, not surprisingly, they want to extend that same kindness to others. Instead of begrudgingly donating to educational institutions, they actively seek out opportunities, asking how they can help. They're not motivated by an ideal, an example of philanthropy, or even a potential tax deduction. They know personally what such charity means to a recipient. They were changed by what they received and they live accordingly.

The same is true of the Christian life. Jesus doesn't call you to do anything for someone else that he has not already done for you. Jesus expects you to forgive others because you already know what it is to be forgiven. You know what it is to owe far more than you could ever hope to pay and have God cancel your debt. In response, he now directs you to cancel the debts that others ring up. True, other people do not deserve to be forgiven, but then again, neither did you. Forgiving others is hard work, but it was hard work for Jesus too, and you are already the recipient of his efforts. That means you should not feel coerced into forgiving, but you should do so freely and, in some measure, with delight.

Amy repeatedly suffered horrible abuse at the hand of her father in the kind of story that rightly makes your stomach queasy and your blood boil. The repercussions extended far into her adult life and included mental and emotional anguish and a divorce. Yet a strong thread of redemption also runs through her story. Some years ago she wrote her father a letter that essentially said, "You have wronged me and I forgive you because Jesus forgave me." The letter came after years of walking with Jesus and his people, but it came. It came willingly, of her own choosing, because she had experienced the true freedom that only comes from being forgiven.

Living life as a forgiving person – bearing with others, repeatedly seeking their good over the long haul – is supernatural. You only find this attitude in people who have experienced forgiveness themselves. That is the key to understanding what Jesus means when he says, "But if you do not forgive men their sins, your Father will not forgive your sins."[17] One indication of whether or not you've been forgiven is how readily and willingly you forgive others. Do you delight to do so because you are simply giving away the mercy you freely received? Or do you have to be forced into it? For many of us, a struggle takes place here. (Remember how few biblical examples there are of people who live this way?) How do you develop a genuine forgiving attitude toward people in general? You go back to the basics.

GROWING IN FORGIVING

First, meditate on how Jesus has forgiven you. Reflect on passages like Psalm 103 and Matthew 18:21-35. Think back over your life and remember how lost you were before you came to faith. But think also of the last few hours and how far short you are from holiness even today. How much do you depend even now on his forgiveness? Give yourself to this type of meditation and you will soon find your heart softening toward those who sin against you. You will rediscover that you and your offender are in the same boat, and you will desire to show him or her the same mercy you have been shown.

Next, think of others who have shown mercy in forgiving you. My wife is an amazing woman in many respects, but perhaps the aspect I most deeply appreciate is that she does not hold a grudge. As the king of grudge holders, I find her lack of bitterness absolutely astounding. She has put up with a critical, prickly, insecure husband for nearly fifteen years – and she's still nice to me! She's not a fool – she knows what I'm like – but she does not remind me of the ways I've sinned against her. She literally keeps no record of wrongs. I know of no one like her.

Can you imagine the effect she has had on me? Her longsuffering forgiveness has allowed me to grow up by making a safe place for me to face my flaws and failings. I have felt less need to hide them. Instead,

---

17 Matt. 6:15.

I've been able to deal with them in a way that has matured and softened me. You too have people in your life whose forgiveness has helped to reshape you in God-ward directions. Have you considered what it would be like for you to play such a role in someone else's life?

Finally, think about how "stuck" other people are, so that you grow in pity for them instead of becoming hardened against them. It's an awful thing to be sinned against seventy times, but it's even worse to be the one committing the same sin seventy times. What a wretched thing it is to be stuck! To constantly interrupt others, to feel compelled to draw attention to yourself, and to watch life slip away because of your own laziness or lack of planning. How hard it is to find yourself internally breaking your marriage vows every time a pretty woman walks by, to be ceaselessly critical, constantly suspicious, or regularly harsh with your children. We may experience the difficulty of having to forgive, but the person being forgiven struggles with a life that is out of control. If you think about what habitual sinning is like for the other person, you'll find your heart going out to him. You'll find yourself wanting to forgive him. Often the catalyst for forgiveness is a tender appreciation of someone else's weaknesses.

No one will be able to prove scientifically that forgiveness is as necessary to life as food and water. But its absence produces the same effect on the spirit as withholding nourishment does on the body. Without forgiveness you could neither survive your own sin nor endure the effects of interacting with other sinners – redeemed or not. You would either coldly turn inward, shutting yourself off from others, or violently explode outward, inflicting greater misery than you had received. Both paths destroy relationship. Only the grace of forgiveness can overcome them. If you know what it is to be pardoned by the Father, then you will grow in forgiving others.

on your own

 Think about the areas in your life where you struggle to forgive someone seven times, much less seventy times seven. Which things are hardest for you to forgive? These may be difficulties you encounter with everyone, or they may be more connected to a specific individual who has repeatedly sinned against you.

2 Identify the ways in which you typically withhold forgiveness. Do you hold grudges? Do you explode in angry tirades? Perhaps you change the subject when someone asks forgiveness, or you simply avoid and ignore those who have wronged you. How do you fight against forgiving?

3 Ask yourself, *Are there people in my life I've not forgiven?* An easy test is to ask, *What pops into my mind when I think about a certain person?* If you cannot think of a person without thinking of his sin against you, it's a safe bet that you haven't forgiven him.

4 Now the hard parts. (Let me warn you: this first part is humbling.) Ask Jesus to forgive you for not forgiving. Be sure to include the people involved as well as your patterns of non-forgiveness. Ask him for the grace to forgive them in your own heart (Mark 11:25) and then do so. Next, seriously consider whether you need to initiate a conversation with anyone at this time regarding how he or she has wronged you. If you were wronged long ago, you may need to ask a friend or pastor what would be wise for you to do at this point.

Are you growing in serving others?

Sin ruins everything. It prevents us from worshiping and enjoying our God. It also keeps us from enjoying and helping his people – our family. Our relationships everywhere are strained and estranged. Part of God's work on earth involves reversing the relational pollution caused by sin. As you develop confidence in your God – moving closer to him, trusting him to purify you – you also move closer to his people. Your relationships taste more of redemption. You long to connect with others in meaningful ways. You want to care for them. You want to serve. Such desires come when you experience God moving toward you.

HIDING FROM SINFUL TEMPTATIONS?

Too often, however, we unwittingly undermine those desires by believing that our sinful inclinations are stronger than God's commitment to transform us. Years ago I read a story about a gifted pastor. He had good insight into the Scriptures and spoke powerfully; his congregation felt very blessed by his ministry. When he retired, a younger man asked the pastor why he had not sought to use his gifts in a wider sphere of influence. The older man explained that he'd realized early in his life that he loved being known, recognized, and respected. Because of that latent pride, he had avoided opportunities that might have fed his sense of self-importance. The story was presented as an example of a humble man who knew his limitations and wisely did not put himself in places where he would be easily tempted.

Certainly the pastor was humble, but I found myself wondering how the kingdom of God might have advanced if this man had approached his problem differently. I know how dangerous it is to speculate about a person you do not know but, staying mindful of that concern, ask with me, "What effect might the pastor have had on the kingdom if he had spent more time fighting his arrogance than guarding against it?"

Lest you think it's inappropriate to ask that question, consider that Aaron had to wrestle with the same kind of thoughts when he was consecrated as Israel's high priest. He'd been forgiven by God for fulfilling the Israelites' desires for visible gods. Then God put him in a place where he was called to lead them and not be led by them – a place full of temptation for him. If you followed the lead of the retiring pastor, you might be tempted to advise Aaron, "You know, Aaron, you've already demonstrated that you don't have what it takes to stand up to people and do or say what they need. You're happier giving in to what others want than you are leading them in godliness. Maybe you shouldn't put yourself once more in a place where you can be so easily tempted."

Certainly the apostle Peter wrestled with such advice. After holding a front row seat through Jesus' ministry years – seeing the miracles, hearing the teaching, witnessing the Transfiguration, being renamed "rock" – he denied Christ. That will disqualify you from ministry like little else! Can you hear him wrestling with himself? *What will keep me from denying Christ again when the heat gets turned up? How can I represent him after what I've done?* So he announces, "I'm going out to fish."[1] At best, he was unsure about his present calling, so he turned, unfocused and ambivalent, to a trade he knew well. At worst, he was leaving the ministry and resuming his former occupation. Jesus had promised that he would learn to catch men, but in his fearfulness, Peter was more caught than catcher. At least fish didn't frighten him!

Aaron and Peter faced the same questions: *Can I hope to live differently so that I serve God well, or will I keep falling into the same pit? Am I doomed to continue being led by the thoughts and opinions of others?* If these men could not hope to overcome their temptations, it would be best to avoid them, even if it meant avoiding ministry opportunities.

Their lives invite you to consider what lies beyond being reconciled with God and having him remove the crushing burden of your sins. Is it possible to actually live differently or will you be stuck doing the same things over and over?

---

[1] John 21:3.

Thank God that when he pursues you, he intends his involvement in your life to transform you. He works on you on the inside, but those interior changes spread outward to affect every part of your life, including a desire to serve others.

TRANSFORMING GRACE

In the lives of these two men, notice how atonement leads to a restoration of their service to God and others. Both needed to have their sin debt paid so that they could serve. Moses offered a sacrifice to atone for Aaron and his sons' sins and subsequently ordained them.[2] Aaron's past failures were not permitted to disqualify him from the priestly service to which God had called him.

Jesus himself offered the sacrifice to atone for Peter's faithlessness. Even though he had warned Peter that he would deny him, Jesus still atoned for him on the cross. He remained faithful despite Peter's faithlessness. After his resurrection, Jesus pursued Peter.[3] He went looking for his lost sheep and found him. He took Peter aside, asking him three times – one for each denial – "Do you love me?" Each time Peter affirmed his love, Jesus reaffirmed his ministry calling by directing him to "feed my sheep." Jesus addressed Peter's failure in a way that gave him a second chance.

These men were not set aside while others took their place. Instead, God canceled the debts they owed him and continued his plan to use them as his chosen leaders. But how well did these men carry out their callings? What effect did atonement and restoration have on their lives?

Initially for Aaron, it didn't look like much had changed. God confronted him a little later when he and Miriam grumbled about the honor that Moses received over them.[4] Since Miriam bore the brunt of God's punishment and Aaron only received a rebuke, it appears that, yet again, Aaron had followed someone else's lead into sin. Not an auspicious start for the newly pardoned high priest! But this time, Aaron did something he did not do at Sinai. When he saw the severity of Miriam's punishment, he interceded for his sister. He began living as a high priest and he spoke up to ease her punishment. Here you see the emerging fruit of a transformed life. Aaron began to change.

That change continued. Later, when the Israelites resisted his and Moses' leadership, Aaron fell on his face and interceded for them, not once but multiple times.[5] He grew into his role as an intercessor

---

2 Lev. 8-9, especially 8:14-21.
3 John 21:1-19.
4 Num. 12.
5 Num. 14:5; 16:22; 20:6.

appointed by God for the people.[6] When God sent a plague, Aaron ran to get his censer, filled it with incense and made atonement for the people. He stood right in the middle of the plague – the best place to be if you wanted to die – and the plague halted where Aaron was standing. Having been cleansed himself, Aaron became a leader who interceded for the Israelites when they sinned. He did not join in their rebellion but sought to remove the gap between them and God that their rebellion created.

You see the same transformation in Peter as he grew into his role as spokesman for the disciples. He explained to the crowd gathered for Pentecost what the coming of the Holy Spirit meant. He healed and preached at the temple and even more bravely spoke to the authorities who had terrified him two months earlier.[7] He defied the Jewish Council's warning to stop preaching the gospel, and even after he was beaten and imprisoned, he spread the good news of what Jesus had accomplished.[8]

Aaron grew from being a people pleaser to an intercessor. Peter went from denying Christ to boldly proclaiming him. These men changed from being afraid of people to being afraid *for* people, realizing that, if they did not act, the people around them would suffer dire consequences. The fear that previously had driven them to yield to people's desires was replaced by a supernatural concern for their welfare. They were compelled to act for other people's best interests even when those interests went against their own. The grace that removed their sins also transformed their primary motivation.

TRANSFORMED MINISTRY

Earlier, Aaron and Peter had been motivated by a fear of people. Fear can either lead you to retreat from others ("I don't want you to hurt me") or fawn all over them ("I need you to be happy with me"). Both sides of this people-pleasing desire put others in charge of what we do and say. We allow others to dictate when and how we're involved in their lives, which often leads to feeling used and manipulated. We describe it as being a doormat – lying down and letting other people walk all over us. Clearly, that is not what Jesus intends when he calls us to serve others.

---

[6] Num. 16:41-48.
[7] Acts 2:14-4:22.
[8] Acts 5:17-42.

One popular solution to this problem teaches people to stand up for themselves by learning to say "No!" to unwanted intrusions. While that sounds good, most of these approaches view others only as encroaching threats, resulting in a pendulum swing to the opposite extreme. Instead of being scared of others and doing what they want, people harden themselves. They turn down legitimate requests for help along with the illegitimate ones. No longer ruled by another person's agenda, they find themselves ruled by their own. They become the final authority on when and how to help. Figure 20-1 illustrates these two opposing ways to wrongly react when others want our help.

●————————————————————————————●

Man-pleaser
(I serve when and how *you* want)

Me-pleaser
(I serve when and how *I* want)

Figure 20-1

Jesus calls us to something different. When he calls us to serve, he disrupts our plans and agendas, but he does not place us at someone else's beck and call. Instead, we serve at his call. I am called to do what Jesus thinks is good for you – not what I alone think is good for you, nor what you alone think I should do. At times I will help you with what you're doing or give you tangible resources or encouragement. At other times, I will not help because to do so would inappropriately enable you to stay stuck in patterns that hurt you. Sometimes I may even need to rebuke you – something neither of us enjoys – in order to serve you best. Serving Christ by helping you means that you don't call the shots and neither do I. Instead, I adjust my life for your benefit as Jesus defines "benefit."

Figure 20-2 shows us that Christ's call is not simply a compromise between two bad motivations. It is a completely different motivation altogether. I no longer decide whether or not to get involved based on a human agenda. I make that decision based on what my Lord would have me do. In that sense, all of us must see our calling as something that stands apart from the contrasting reactions of Figure 20-1.[9]

_____

[9] I am indebted to David Powlison for this diagram, which illustrates the difference between two opposing ungodly positions and a godly position.

Whether we're too quick to help others or too quick to resist helping others, God always calls us to a third way – to move toward Jesus – where we serve others for their godly benefit.

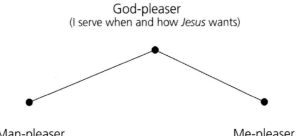

God-pleaser
(I serve when and how *Jesus* wants)

Man-pleaser
(I serve when and how *you* want)

Me-pleaser
(I serve when and how *I* want)

Figure 20-2

Obviously, discerning Christ's call requires great wisdom, but developing that ability is possible for God's people. As you watch Aaron and Peter's lives, you see them both grow in their understanding of what people need. After Jesus restores him, Peter speaks up even though his words will be unpopular: he has to serve Jesus, not men. Aaron's life is dedicated to helping people get right with God – according to God's perspective, not theirs. God does not atone for these men so that they can retire from ministry, licking their wounds in regret. His atonement produces an internal transformation that expresses itself in their willingness to serve for the benefit of others. Two people-fearers who served their own agendas were transformed by God into God-fearers who served others well.

TRANSFORMATION: ALREADY AND NOT YET

Notice, however, that their transformations didn't take place overnight, nor were they complete in this life. Both Aaron and Peter could still be tempted and led astray. Along with Moses, Aaron rebelled against God's command to speak to the rock to produce water.[10] Peter reverted to people-pleasing when he abruptly stopped eating with his Gentile brothers because members of the circumcision party showed up.[11]

---

[10] Num. 20:12, 24-25.
[11] Gal. 2:11-14.

Change, while it certainly takes place for those who have experienced atonement, is not necessarily easy, quick, or complete.

Too often we measure change in high jump terms: the only thing that matters is whether or not you go over the bar. It doesn't matter how much you practice. It doesn't matter what your form looks like. It doesn't even matter how many trial runs up to the bar you take. The only thing of any importance is whether or not you sail over the bar without knocking it off.

Growth in holiness is not like that. Transforming change takes time and practice. Each time you get a little better, it comes a little more easily, and you feel more confident. Practice and perseverance count because the Christian life involves growth in holiness, not simply its ultimate attainment. A faithful life – a successful life – is measured by far more than the end result.

I once taught a week-long seminar that didn't go well the first day. People seemed bored, which is death for a speaker. The feedback I received was not positive, and the questions people asked were very different from what I had been asked before, all of which unnerved me. This was bad, but my own sins compounded the problem. My twist on the universal problem of fearing people is that I want you to respect me. I don't particularly care if you like me, but if what I say doesn't strike you as the most interesting thing you've ever heard, then I feel I have failed as a teacher. Against that impossibly arrogant standard, the class I was teaching was a decided failure.

Then, help came from a very ironic direction. That same day, I gave an illustration of a time when my desire for respect had gotten out of control. Suddenly I realized that the same dynamics were at work in me all over again! That night, a major portion of my preparation for the following day dealt with my fear about what other people were thinking. I repented over being more concerned with what they thought of me than what they thought of God. I realized (again!) that God had not sent me there for people to think well of me. He wanted people to think well of *him* and to be helped in their lives and ministries. So I asked him to change me and make me more concerned for what the group needed. As I prayed, I felt a change take place inside.

I lost my obsessive anxiety over what my students were thinking and spent the next few hours making changes to the schedule that focused on benefiting the class instead of my reputation. I woke up the next morning well rested and looking forward to teaching. I was no longer scared. I continued to remind myself to work for the students, not for their admiration. The next several days were much better – and, as a nice but not necessary bonus, the students thought so too.

That story illustrates a mental picture that my friend Bill Oldham once gave me. He said, "I want the path out of the pit to be as well worn as the path into the pit." Being cleansed from your sins familiarizes you with the path out of the pit. You sense more intuitively when you are responding wrongly: *Oh, here I am again!* You more quickly identify the source of your problem, acknowledge what you are doing wrong, and run to Jesus for help. You become more confident in Christ's love for you and his desire to help you live a holy life. You better understand what to do to handle your sins and failures. Even the time between your failures lengthens so that you are less frequently tripped up. God not only brings conviction and gives grace, he also changes *you*.

God's kingdom has been moving forward since Jesus first announced its breakthrough into time and space. It has extended itself around the globe and worked deeply in hundreds of millions of people over thousands of years. Despite numerous setbacks, it is neither slowing down nor retreating. Although its advance is energized by the Spirit, God chooses to use his people to carry his work forward. Most often he chooses to use the weak and foolish – Aaron, Peter, you, and me – to shame the strong.

God pursues you. He does not treat you as you deserve. He provides you with his resources and transforms you. He does all this because he wants you to know and love him. He also wants you to have the joy-filled privilege of partnering with him in building a kingdom that will last forever. If that idea grips you, then embrace with both hands the opportunities he gives you – both to fight with sin and to serve. You will find that such temporal labor will generate riches you'll enjoy and share for eternity.

on your own

1   What areas of giftedness or ministry are compromised by your sin patterns? In what ways are you hindered from caring for others as the Lord calls you to?

2   How do fear and faithlessness hinder your ministry to others? What lies from the enemy keep you from using your gifts to build Christ's kingdom?

3   Where have you seen growth in these areas? Where do you see God using people and circumstances to help you to be different? Ask several friends how they have seen you grow. Ask people to pray for your growth and to check with you in two weeks to see how you're doing.

4   What opportunities to believe and serve are in front of you now? These may be areas that will challenge you, but they will also be experiences God will use to further his work in you. Prayerfully consider pursuing one of these opportunities, knowing that it will stretch you.

SCRIPTURE INDEX